Vietnam
The Way I Saw It

By Warren D. Welch

This Book is Dedicated To
Norman Bruce Welch
1945-2008
Vietnam 1966-67

Many thanks to
John "Mac" McMahon
for his help in remembering
names and other facts that
were used in this book.
His perspective is on page 79.

Many thanks to
Juan A. Maldonado II
for his help in editing this book

Copyright © 2014 by Warren D. Welch
All Rights Reserved
ISBN: 978-1-304-79429-1

Vietnam
The Way I Saw It

Table of Contents

Page	Title
1	Beginning of my Military Adventure
7	Adventures in Paradise
11	Vietnam Bound
17	Arrival at Cu Chi
25	Security Comes First
31	What's Going on Here?
33	Back to Situation Normal
37	Work Assignment Cu Chi
51	R&R and Other Fun Activities
59	My Tour Comes to an End
63	Company C Roster 1966-67
65	Fun at Fort Hood
74	Calendar Pictures
75	In Conclusion
77	Cu Chi Map
78	Vietnam Map
79	John "Mac" McMahon – A Cook's Perspective

BEGINNING OF MY MILITARY ADVENTURE

In 1964 I was 20 years old; President Kennedy had just been assassinated in November of 1963, and I was in my second year at the University of Denver as a mechanical engineering major. I didn't really know what I wanted to do with my life, and by the Christmas holiday, I had dropped out of school and was trying figure things out. I knew that as soon as my draft board got news of my dropping out of school, I faced getting drafted (this was prior to the draft lottery, and local draft boards sent idle or trouble-making teens off to the military). At the time there was no appreciable anti-war movement, and most citizens still believed that the government was doing the right thing. My mother, who lived in Philadelphia, was expecting me for Christmas, and on the drive back East with some of my fraternity brothers, we stopped off in Jamestown, NY to spend the night at Dave Santuary's home. I can remember the horror and chastisement from Dave's mother as we had dinner that night. Both his parents were dismayed that I hadn't shared my news with my parents, but the reality was that I had basically been left to my own devices since I was 17 years old. Now don't get me wrong here; I was still getting monetary support from my dad, but he lived in England; and my mom, who had walked out on her family in England and flown back to the U.S., wasn't a trusted confidant. After Christmas I was still staying with my mother and half heartedly attempting to get a job. I managed to get a job as an estimator, but the job only lasted a week, so in February of 1965 I enlisted in the Army for my 21st birthday present.

Prior to my enlistment I had no work ethic as I had never had to work hard for anything. I had gone through my teens with no sense of urgency or purpose. I had bad school grades, had never held a job beyond a month, and life was just one big party. Just before I went to Basic Training, my mother and I went to see the James Bond movie, *Goldfinger*, in downtown Philadelphia. My mother, who was recently divorced, couldn't stop laughing about and bringing up the name "Pussy Galore" from the movie. When I was assigned my military ID number (prior to using Social Security Numbers), the sergeant said to me, "Welch, your number is RA13845 double "O" seven, licensed to kill", referencing the James Bond character. The sergeant who issued the ID numbers told us that our number would become etched into our brain, and at 70 years old I can still rattle my RA13845007 off like it was 1965.

I had received the highest score in my group on the enlistment test, so the Army saw fit to put me in charge of the 100 plus enlistees and draftees along with all their paperwork for the train trip from Philadelphia, Pennsylvania to Columbia, South Carolina. When we got to Washington, DC, we had a 3 hour layover while we switched to a train with sleeper cars. We were all supposed to stay in the train station, but there was a group of my charges that wanted to see Washington, and they weren't listening to me. I remember trying to stay calm, but inside I was flipping out because I could see me getting in trouble upon arrival at Columbia because one of the partying recruits had missed the train. Thankfully everyone made it back for the train departure, and we were off looking for Army adventure. We had all gone to sleep, when the train hit a truck at a crossing and had to stop for a while. When we finally got back to sleep, we all envisioned sleeping late the next morning before we reached Columbia around noon. At 06:00 AM the porter came around, woke us all up, and told us to make up our berths. We all protested, but he forcefully replied that we belonged to the Army now and we better get used to getting up early. We all reluctantly got up and complied with his request before heading to the dining car. We were greeted in Columbia by a group of buses and drill instructors who immediately started whipping us into shape when we got off the train. Line up, do this, do that, "move your ass" was all we heard while we were herded onto the buses.

I took my Basic Training at Fort Jackson, South Carolina, and I really didn't know what I was in for. The first couple days were spent getting a physical exam, shots, a buzz haircut, uniforms, equipment, and settled into our barracks. I got examined for and fitted with my Army issue black plastic rimmed glasses, and they ordered prescription lens inserts for my gas mask. Our drill sergeant was a 5 foot 4 inch tall, 140 pound Puerto Rican Sergeant First Class E-7 who was probably in his late 30s. Most of us recruits didn't think he was the brightest bulb in the box, but he was one of those wiry little guys you wouldn't want to mess with and he demanded your respect. The last thing anyone wanted was having this drill sergeant calling you out during our daily training. More than one of the recruits was tempted to take him on because of his small stature, but the sergeant made it abundantly clear to them that it would be a fools mission. After a very harrowing first day we were all exhausted and looking forward to a good night's sleep. At 0530 the next morning we were rudely awakened by our drill sergeant, and given 10 minutes to get in uniform before going on a pre-breakfast 3 mile run. Of course I was at the back of the pack with the drill sergeant yelling after me, "Welch, move that 'fat' ass!" At 180+ pounds, I was overweight and out of shape, so anything physical was difficult for me at first. Trips to the mess hall were preceded with lots of physical training (PT), and you had to swing through 50 feet of monkey bars before they would let you enter the mess hall. I wore a size small shirt at the time, and with my weight, anything involving upper body strength was my downfall. That first week I was wondering if I was even going to make it through the bars so I could get to eat. Next I got blisters on my hands from the monkey bars and the pain really started when the blisters broke. This kid had a lot of toughening up to do. When we finally got into the mess area to eat we were given less than 10 minutes to finish before we were run off to go participate in more military training.

In Basic Training the kiss of death was being sent back because you couldn't keep up or got sick; no recruit wanted to repeat Basic with a new group. Back before I enlisted in the Army, I invariably got sick with bronchitis every winter and this year was no exception. Almost 3 weeks into Basic I got sick, but after some penicillin shots and 2 days in the infirmary I was returned to duty. Unfortunately, because of my illness, I missed the part of weapons training where you sight in your M-14 rifle and get to practice shooting at targets. I went from getting out of the infirmary to taking my first trip to the rifle range to qualify with my weapon. My dad had never owned or fired a weapon while I knew him, but I had fired .22 rifles on several occasions with my friends and their parents. At the range we were firing from the prone position at metal human silhouettes that would pop up and fall back down when you hit them or time ran out. I had never experienced firing a rifle like an M-14 with 7.62mm ammunition, yet here I was,

Marksman Badge

qualify or get sent back, hoping I was hitting enough targets. Fortunately I was able to barely qualify as a Marksman, which was minimum qualification. After leaving Basic Training I never again had occasion to fire my assigned weapon, even while I was in Vietnam.

One of my personal flaws that manifested itself during Basic was my excitability when I was placed in a stressful situation. I didn't tend to function in a predictable manner when placed in these situations, and this fact was to put me in peril later on in Vietnam. We had training for one day with hand grenades where we learned about the parts, how to remove the 5 second fuse, and how to throw one at a target.

One of the specific exercises we performed was to run up to a bunker, flop on the ground beside the bunker's weapon opening, pull the pin on the grenade, release the arming lever, and wait for 3 seconds before dropping it into the bunker opening. Now these were only practice grenades, but they looked real and had realistic pins, levers, and fuses, as well as making loud fire cracker noises when they went off. I remember that I flubbed this portion of training by dropping the grenade in the opening almost immediately after releasing the arming lever. Like I said, stress made me very excitable. The last station at grenade training was throwing a live grenade at a target while kneeling behind a sandbag wall. The range sergeant obviously saw something me he didn't like and declined to let me participate in the live throw. I recall being upset about this, but maybe it was for the best as a worse case scenario would have me pulling the pin, releasing the lever, and then just dropping the grenade.

We spent a lot of time doing drills with our M-14s like they had bayonets on them. This was like a karate kata routine being performed with a rifle. We constantly repeated the same routine of parries, thrusts, and butt strokes until it became second nature to us. We spent one afternoon pairing off with pugil sticks (4 foot poles with heavy padding on either end) that are used to simulate a bayonet fight with the enemy. We were informed that in real battle an average bayonet fight took less than 2 seconds of contact to determine the winner, and here the winners were the participants that rushed in with their sticks flashing. Just from observing, you realized that this was not something for the weak and timid; pure aggression was winning the day. Once you took a step back, you were finished. I got my ass kicked that day.

One evening I was selected to pull guard duty at the enlisted men's club, and this involved maintaining order amongst the soldiers who were there enjoying their down time. The soldiers in the club were not Basic trainees, but soldiers that were assigned to regular duty at Fort Jackson. We were given Army issue pump shotguns with 15" barrels (an illegal sawed off shotgun in civilian life) for performing this duty with, but of course we were not given any ammunition. If there was a fight or riot at the club, our orders were to put our back to the wall and start using prods and butt strokes with the empty weapon just like bayonet training had taught us. Thank goodness nothing happened during my watch, and I didn't have to make an ass out of myself.

Basic Training involves learning how to lead a disciplined life; following orders, marching in formation, cleaning and firing your weapon, and learning the warrior trade. As the weeks pass by, you fall into the routine and the physical side gets easier. Back in the 60s this was a man's army, and there were no verbal restrictions on what the sergeants could do to try to break you down. I wore black plastic rimmed glasses and with my big ass physical shape, some of the training sergeants would call me every vulgar name in the book. It's a good thing I had thick skin and was used to ignoring people that tried to bully or belittle me. Towards the end of Basic we went on a 20 mile forced march at night through the South Carolina sandy soil; one step forward followed by slipping ¼ step back. I remember a sense of pride when we'd completed this march because 20 miles is difficult, but in the dark of night it's damn difficult. When I finally finished Basic Training, I can recall a great sense of accomplishment as we passed in review at our graduation ceremony.

In 1965 a draftee had 2 years of active duty to fulfill and a first time enlistee would have volunteered for 3 years. As you first entered the Army you were assigned the rank of private E-1 and got paid the grand sum of $83.20 a month. Completion of Basic Training meant a promotion to private E-2 and $85.80 per month. From then on advancement was based on merit and when slots were allocated to the unit you were assigned to. The ranks immediately above E-2 were private first class (PFC), E-3 and specialist 4 (SP4) E-4, which paid $117.90 and $165.50 respectively starting in August of 1965. A soldier received additional pay if they were married and after they had completed 2 years of service. Personnel serving in a war zone like Vietnam also received hazardous duty pay of $55.00 per month. Payday was once a month and we got paid in cash that was placed in a small manila envelope. Everyone was running around with full wallets on payday, but a private's pay didn't go very far. The best part was that all your basic needs like food and shelter were taken care of, so how you spent your money was entirely up to you. If you ran out of money you just had to stay put in the barracks until the next payday came along, or find some other soldier to borrow money from.

When I enlisted in Philadelphia I had wanted to work with computers, but had been persuaded to sign on as an Artillery Repairman which had a job MOS (Military Occupation Code) of 45C20. I took my AIT (Advanced Individual Training) at the Aberdeen Proving Ground in Aberdeen, Maryland which was far superior to Basic Training because the mess halls were staffed by civilians and there was no KP. We also received an hour for lunch away from classes, and there were lots of downtime activities on base. The movie *Cat*

Ballou starring Jane Fonda and Lee Marvin was playing on base, and my classmate, who served in the Wisconsin Marine Reserve, and I went to see it. We both laughed so hard that we just had to see the movie again. How were we to know what Jane Fonda would eventually become? My Marine classmate was always complaining that the Navy bought them all the Army's left over equipment leaving the Army with the latest and greatest. His reserve unit had 8 inch howitzers that were towed behind a truck, while the Army had the much newer tracked, self propelled version of this weapon. I really got into the training at Aberdeen, and prided myself on how fast I could disassemble and then reassemble the breech mechanisms on 105mm and 155mm howitzers. I especially enjoyed learning new things in the classroom and would become mesmerized by the lecturer talking to us. We also learned about other weapons that I would never again come into contact with like the M-289 "Honest John" rocket launcher, and the M-28 "Davy Crockett" nuclear device launcher that had a range of $1\frac{1}{4}$ miles. Who would be crazy enough to set off a nuclear explosion that was only $1\frac{1}{4}$ miles from your firing position? The artillery repair training lasted 8 weeks and I graduated at the top of my class. The top performer in the class before me had been assigned to instructor duty at Aberdeen, and I fantasized that this would be great non-hazardous duty for this kid. When I eventually got my orders I sure was in for a surprise; I had been assigned to serve in Paradise.

I had gone to high school for a couple years in England at Bushy Park High School which is a military dependant school, and because my dad was an engineer working for a British firm, he had to pay tuition so I could attend. One of my best friends at Bushy Park was Norman "Happy" Chalmers whose dad was a Captain in the Navy, and while I was still at Aberdeen I had made plans to travel to Virginia Beach to spend Easter with Hap and his family. For some unrecalled reason I made the decision to not make the trip and didn't even call them to let them know I wasn't coming. When I eventually talked with Hap's mother some 30 years later she recalled the event, expressed her disappointment, and wouldn't even give me Hap's phone number. I eventually reconnected with Hap through email obtained from the Bushy Park web site, but one of my big regrets in life was that I had just given up on a friendship that should have been for a lifetime.

Schofield Barracks, Hawaii — U. S. Army Photo

ADVENTURES IN PARADISE

My first duty assignment was the 725th Maintenance Battalion (Motto: "Service to the Line") of the 25th Infantry Division (Tropic Lightning), and I was transported by troop ship from the Oakland Army Terminal to Pearl Harbor in Hawaii. Most soldiers would have gotten a plane ticket, but I got a slow Liberty Ship to Paradise. How lucky was I getting stationed in Hawaii for my first assignment; truly dreams are made of this! After my arrival I was assigned to Company C which was quartered at Schofield Barracks. During my first week I was put through more physical and dental exams, as well as receiving more shots for who knows what; I think they were going shot crazy in trying to protect us from every conceivable disease. During my dental exam they determined that I needed many old fillings replaced and that my four wisdom teeth also needed extracting. Sitting in the chair for hours to handle the fillings was bad enough, but when they'd finished with the fillings, they scheduled my wisdom teeth surgery for 06:00 the next morning. In civilian life most dentists would pull 2 wisdom teeth per visit, but the Army was always in a hurry to do things. The Army dentist pulled all 4 of my wisdom teeth; having to split one into 4 parts with a chisel to get it extracted. After all that, his assistant gave me a slip of paper saying I had permission to return to the barracks and rest until noon. A couple days later food got impacted into one of the empty tooth sockets, and the side of my face swelled up like a balloon. Another trip to the dentist and some penicillin shots cleared up this problem. The Army was always in a hurry to give penicillin shots because pills just didn't act fast enough. I will say one thing about Army dentistry; most of my fillings from 1965 didn't have to be replaced until 2010 or 45 years later.

The talk in the barracks was that we were going to be held in reserve for Vietnam in case something big happened there, yet we continued to take jungle warfare related training almost every day. It was fun rappelling off the training tower, but climbing down rope netting into a dummy landing craft was challenging, and mongoose stew was not what I had in mind for dinner. I didn't feel like I had enough on my plate so I volunteered to become a truck driver, and after training on a deuce and a half truck (2 ½ ton), I finally received my military truck driving license.

During my first months in Hawaii I managed to get promoted to Private First Class which meant I must be doing something right. Along with the promotion came a raise in pay to approximately $120 per month; this was only good for one or two trips to town every month because Honolulu was an expensive place for a private in the Army. One Saturday, Guy Easton and I got into civilian clothes and took the bus to Honolulu so we could look around and explore. All the Army troops were warned that the bars on Hotel Street were off limits, so we headed to the area around Waikiki Beach. We walked through the Hilton Hotel, peered into the theater where Don Ho was scheduled to entertain that evening, and crossed the street that ran along the beach to check out the International Market Place where the famous Don the Beachcomber's restaurant was. That evening we walked along Waikiki Beach at Fort DeRussy and I observed how austere the military property was when compared to the civilian areas along the beach. Because of the prices in Honolulu we were almost completely relegated to using affordable on base entertainment, but the Army wasn't giving us too much spare time for that.

Hawaii had just become a state in 1959 and many items like cars were very expensive on the island when compared to the mainland. One of the SP4 soldiers in the barracks at Schofield actually had a car. It was a black 1954 Chevrolet 2 door sedan with a 6

Jungle Warfare training with Company C, 725th Maintenance at Oahu, Hawaii

cylinder, 3-speed on the column that he had paid $400 for. He had purchased it from a soldier who was being transferred, and when it became his turn to leave, he would probably just find another soldier that was willing to pay him the same $400 just to have access to a car. The car was stored off base, and I don't know how they handled the title transfer and insurance on the vehicle, but knowing transient soldiers, these details probably weren't of too much concern. All of us base restricted privates were jealous of the mobility he had in exploring Oahu.

I was used to little cockroaches from back home, but the barracks at Schofield had the large flying variety that liked to bombard the TV light source while we were watching the black and white TV in our barrack's common area. I can recall shaving at the sink one morning when a huge cockroach came strolling out from behind the metal mirror like he owned the place. The barracks were infested and they were trying all kinds of pesticides, but nothing they did made a dent in the population. I got assigned to KP a couple of times and could never figure why we had to hand-peel potatoes when they had a machine to do the job. We would clean the kitchen after meals by putting on rubber boots and flooding the kitchen floor with 6 inches of water before scrubbing everything and flushing it down the drain.

Only weeks away being deployed to Vietnam from Schofield Barracks in Hawaii
(Notice the M-12 blank firing attachments on the M-14 rifles)

In October Company C made an overnight sea voyage in a flat-bottom landing craft to the Big Island of Hawaii to take further warfare training at the Pohakuloa Military Reserve which is located in the valley between the Mauna Kea and Mauna Loa volcanoes. They warned us that we were likely to get sea sick because flat bottom boats weren't the smoothest ride on the open sea. When we landed the next morning, we off-loaded all our trucks and equipment and took everything to a staging area. Before we started traveling to the training area, they let us go swimming by the LST landing area in the 90 degree water. I was used to the frigid water off the coast of Maine and to me this was like taking a warm bath.

All our deuce and a half trucks were well used Korean War vintage with gasoline engines and automatic transmissions. Many of the trucks broke down or overheated on a regular basis. The drive up to our destination at altitude was accented by many trucks dropping off and having to be serviced by the wrecker with the mechanics that trailed the convoy. Those that broke down were gratified that the wrecker was one of the Army's new reliable versions with a diesel engine.

The big surprise for me was fall on the Big Island at altitude which saw temperatures in the forties. This definitely was not the Hawaii that I pictured in my mind. Our barracks were Quonset huts left over from World War II and we were drawn to their heaters and warm shelter at night. One day we got to convoy through volcanic dust that was two feet deep; the only good vehicle was the first one in the convoy as everyone behind ate ground up pumice. Another day, I recall being up on the side of a highly vegetated hillside and looking across eyeball to eyeball with F100 pilots as they flew down through the valleys during the training exercise. It was almost like you could reach out and touch the jet-planes as they flew by. One pilot looked over at me and gave me the thumbs up as he flew by.

In December we were issued new trucks and some of us started to wonder if something was in the wind. These deuce and a half trucks were right off the assembly line, had straight-6 diesel multi-fuel engines with 427 cubic-inch displacement, 5 speed manual transmissions, high and low range, and a transfer box with all 10 wheels driven as an option. These were real trucks that would prove to be very reliable.

On day I was called out of formation by my sergeant and informed that I had been selected to take 60 hours of medical training. I learned how to give CPR, handle sucking wounds, stop bleeding, use tourniquets, and was told to be innovative when it came to saving my fellow soldiers if the time should arise. Christmas of 1965 was approaching and we were now informed that we were to ship out to Vietnam on the 28th of December. The Army put a gag order in place referencing our impending departure and we couldn't even tell our families where and when we were going. Prior to our departure, all our white items were dyed olive drab; we filled out our will and other papers, and everyone made sure their military $10,000 life insurance policy was in order. We also started taking a monthly regimen of shots for obscure tropical diseases. By the time I left the Army, I had accumulated over 30 shots on my record, but it seemed to me like I'd received over 100.

James Peck was my First Sergeant in Hawaii and for my first few months in Vietnam. He was an imposing figure around 40 years old who stood about 6 feet 2 inches tall and shaved his head bald. He was demanding like most NCOs are, but most of us felt he was fair and we respected him for this. While I was in Hawaii they had tested some of us to see if we could qualify for Officer Candidate School (OCS). One afternoon my sergeant informed me that I had passed the testing and could request being transferred to OCS for officer training (90 day wonder). By this time I knew we were going to Vietnam, so at my earliest opportunity I informed First Sergeant Peck that I was requesting to go to OCS training. He simply replied to me, "You really don't want to do that!", and that was the end of that conversation. As a PFC, the Army had taught me to follow orders, so without filing a complaint with the IG (Inspector General), my fate was sealed. To this day I don't know if he was concerned that I wouldn't have made a good candidate, or just didn't want the hassle of finding a new artillery repairman to go to Vietnam with them. I also wonder if I didn't have an ulterior motive in wanting to go to OCS as a means of putting off going to Vietnam. As things worked out, I'm glad I didn't go to OCS.

VIETNAM BOUND

Again I got a WWII era Liberty ship and after slowly crossing the smooth Pacific Ocean, the ship steamed into the South China Sea passing close by the Philippine Islands. We

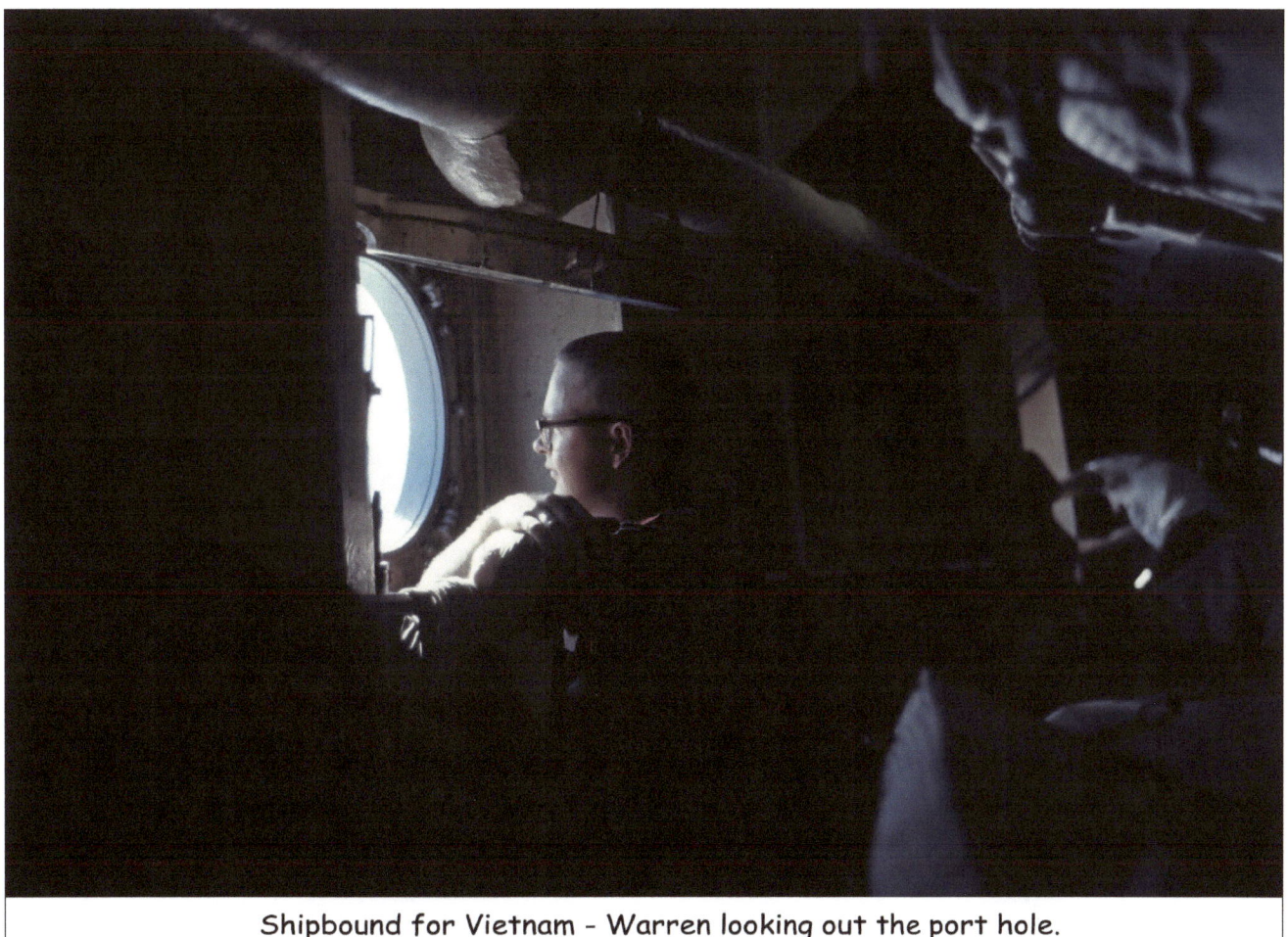
Shipbound for Vietnam - Warren looking out the port hole.

now continued on to Cam Rahn Bay in Vietnam where some of the ship's cargo was off-loaded. On the trip across the Pacific they tried to keep everyone out of trouble and busy by working at some task on the ship. I was assigned to the laundry room which was located below the waterline and had temperatures in excess of 120 degrees. To keep from getting dehydrated we had to work under an air ventilation tube that brought in cool forced air from outside, and to drink water constantly. Life on board the ship was hot, hard work interlaced with daily indoctrination on the Geneva Convention and preparing yourself mentally to kill another human being. After our work day was finished, we all looked forward to spending our evenings overlooking the calm Pacific and watching the flying fish. The compartment where we slept had pipe berths with hammocks that were stacked 4 high. Fortunately we had so few soldiers on board that we each had our own individual hammock and didn't have to put up with anyone sleeping above or below us. One day I went exploring and found at least 2 other rooms that were full of hammocks stacked 4 high. I can only imagine that this would have been pretty uncomfortable during WWII with all the hammocks being full of troops on a trip across the Pacific or the

Sunset on the Pacific - January of 1966

rough North Atlantic. Nineteen days and many miles from Pearl Harbor we arrived at Vung Tau which is located at the mouth of the Saigon River in Vietnam. The Saigon River goes inland to the docks at Saigon which was the major port in Vietnam in 1966. Troops weren't allowed to stay on ships as they went up the river because there was a threat of mines, so we were scheduled to off load the next morning.

Enjoying a peaceful evening on deck in the middle of the Pacific watching the flying fish

First land in many days - Passing by the Philippine Islands

All that first night as we were anchored in the bay at Vung Tau, concussion grenades were periodically thrown into the water to foil any swimmers that were seeking to sabotage the ship. We would just be nodding off to sleep when a grenade would go off and the sound of the explosion echoing off the hull would wake us up. This coupled with the realization that tomorrow we would be going over the side into a landing craft that would take us ashore on Vietnamese soil made for a very stressful night. All of us unseasoned soldiers were excited to get off the ship, but we were very apprehensive about landing on unfamiliar territory in the middle of a war zone. The next morning we boarded the landing craft with our duffle bags and weapons, and after a short trip to the boat ramp, the front ramp on the LST was lowered. There in front of us was a contingent of Army officers and Vietnamese dignitaries to welcome us to Vietnam. The

Stop over at Cam Rahn Bay to unload cargo before heading south to disembark at Vung Tau.

real surprise however was a group of approximately 20 girls wearing white Vietnamese áo dài's (traditional women's clothing that resembles a short dress with a form fitting bodice and slits on the side, and pajama bottoms underneath) and bamboo hats; not the greeting that any of us had envisioned or expected when we were listening to the grenades the previous night. Vietnam was to become a land of many surprises.

We landed at Vung Tau on January 17th, 1966 in the middle of their winter, and the temperature was close to 100 degrees with overwhelming humidity; this definitely was "not" Hawaii. Once we were ashore we marched to a staging area where we loaded into waiting deuce and a half trucks. After driving in a convoy for a couple of hours we arrived at a staging area close to Saigon where we were instructed to pair up, pitch our shelter halves, and dig a protective trench to climb into in case we came under attack. A shelter half is a soldier's individual rain poncho, but when you pair up with a buddy, it's designed to attach together and be used as a basic 2 man shelter to sleep under. We were scheduled to be at the staging area until our ship had unloaded our equipment at Saigon. Pitching the shelter half and blowing up my air mattress was easy, but digging a hole with my entrenching tool when the sun-baked earth was like concrete was next to impossible. We were given empty sand bags to place our excavated soil into, and as we chipped into the hard earth, the sandbags were filled to place along the edge of the trench. After 4 hours of work, you hopefully had a trench that was large enough for you to lie down in with a ring of sand bags that went all around the trench's outer perimeter. Each of us was instructed to dig their own hole, so a person's work ethic was painfully evident at the end of the 4 hours. Some of us had trenches with a wall that was two sand bags high, while others appeared to have barely scraped the surface of the earth. Being in a situation like this made me realize the value of one inch of dirt that was there protecting me from incoming bullets; that one inch of dirt could represent the difference between life and death.

Until we got situated to our new surroundings and situation in Vietnam, our advanced party was guarded by troops that had already been in Vietnam for a while. Our guards at the staging area set up a portable radar unit that we were told would detect any unfriendly Viet Cong that were moving out beyond our encampment's perimeter that night. After picking up our C rations (canned meal packets in a box) and standing evening formation, we settled in for a good night's sleep under the stars in the steamy Vietnamese atmosphere. We had barely closed our eyes when the sound of gunfire erupted from beyond our perimeter, and the sky was alive with red tracers streaming across the sky above us. Everyone immediately dove into their protective trench, and the stress level was immediately ratcheted up a couple more notches. At this point I experienced the worst case of acid stomach I have ever encountered, and how I kept from tossing my cookies is beyond me. When things eventually calmed down, I climbed back under my shelter half only to have the gun fire start again half an hour later. After jumping back and forth a couple of times, I finally decided to spend the rest of the night in my trench. As I look back on the events of this evening, I now realize that this was probably all a set up scenario where the Army attempted to see if you were going to crack under the pressure and be deemed unsuited for the environment we had facing us. At no time during the following year did I ever see another portable radar unit, and I never experienced as much incoming fire as I did that first night on Vietnamese soil.

After that first stressful night, we got up and did our normal morning tasks of washing up and shaving. After eating our breakfast of C-rations, we cleaned up our sleeping area while we awaited our next orders. Wayne Dewberry, another artillery repairman, had just pulled his air mattress out from his shelter when he noticed that there was a snake moving and trying to get away. Now this snake was silver in color, about 3 feet long, and would rear up its head and spread its neck like a cobra when it felt threatened. Now because we were probably staying here for a couple more days, the smart thing to do would be to kill the snake. Apparently GIs just aren't that smart, and they immediately began to play with the snake by poking at it with sticks so it would flare out its neck again. Because of the heat and lack of rain, the earth had large cracks in it, and the next thing we knew the snake had escaped down one of the cracks where we couldn't get to it. I can recall being quite upset because now we were going to have to wonder where the snake was that evening.

After a couple of days, our Liberty Ship went up the Saigon River to the docks and off loaded our trucks and equipment so we could get under way, and convoy to whatever area of Vietnam the Army had in mind for us. As an Artillery Repair Specialist, my truck was loaded with tools and parts that I needed to repair artillery, and when we picked up our trucks from the docks, we checked that nothing was missing before convoying back to the staging area. Statistically about 5 percent of the bombs and artillery shells that the U.S. used in Vietnam were duds, and the Viet Cong liked to find these munitions and make mines from them. They would then bury them in the roads and detonate the mine when we drove over it. Because of the danger from these mines, we covered the entire truck's floorboard, including under the bench seat, with sandbags when we got back to the staging area. We also laid the windshield down flat against the hood of the truck and placed a layer of sandbags across the cowl area. The idea was to stop shrapnel, but if your truck got directly involved with an explosive device those sandbags wouldn't be of much help to you. I was of a mindset where I thought that those sandbags would protect me from just about anything when I was in my truck; how young and foolish I was.

When we traveled in a convoy, I was always assigned another soldier to ride shotgun with me. The Army only assigned an individual one weapon, which for most soldiers in Vietnam, in early 1966 was an M-14 rifle using 7.62mm ammunition. Under the Army's rules of the time, a soldier was also allowed to carry a private weapon as long as it was registered with his company's commanding officer and my first shotgun passenger had his own chrome plated .357 revolver. This was the only time I ever encountered a soldier who had a personal weapon that hadn't been procured in Vietnam, and during all my time in Vietnam, I was never aware of any problems that arose from soldiers that had personal handguns. We kept the revolver lying on the bench seat between us, and I felt like we had an advantage over the trucks that only had their M-14s for protection. As we traveled towards our destination on our first convoy into the Vietnamese countryside, we drove through many small villages. We had been warned that kids had been known to jump up on the step-board of trucks so they could drop an explosive device in, and every town we entered had hoards of kids that liked to race along side our trucks. If one got too close, however, holding up that revolver would make them back off.

After driving for hours, we finally arrived at this large, flat, vegetation-free area where again the sun-baked ground was concrete hard. We parked our trucks in pre-designated spots, prepared the equipment in our trucks for work the next day, and then pitched our shelter halves in preparation for sleep. Most of us didn't know exactly where we were, but the last village we had passed through was Cu Chi that was located 20 miles northwest of Saigon. We later discovered that Cu Chi was on Route 1, the main road from Saigon to Phnom Penh in Cambodia, and Cu Chi also anchored the southern end of the Iron Triangle, a notorious wooded Viet Cong stronghold.

ARRIVAL AT CU CHI

Company C of the 725th Maintenance Battalion was part of an advanced party tasked with setting up a base camp at Cu Chi for the 2nd Brigade of the 25th Infantry Division. The

Sleeping under our shelter halves at Cu Chi when it was a glorified rice paddy
(January 1966 - We lived like this for a couple of months until we got our tent frame kits assembled)

bulk of the 2nd Brigade was slated to arrive later in 1966. The 1st Infantry Division, which was already in-country, provided protection at Cu Chi for the brigade's advanced party until we got situated and were able to protect ourselves. Because we were an advanced party, our company was tasked with both maintenance and supply functions, and we ran a supply convoy into Saigon every day. Additionally, we performed helicopter and aircraft maintenance which usually had its own separate company in a maintenance battalion. Up until 1967 the Army actually had some fixed wing aircraft like the

De Havilland CV-2 Caribou Airplane   U. S. Army Photo

Caribou cargo/paratrooper aircraft in its inventory. This airplane was a STOL (Short Take Off and Landing) aircraft and I was always amazed to see a plane that could carry 32 fully equipped troops come in for a landing on what seemed like an impossibly short landing strip. Caribous had extremely long, ungainly-looking main landing gear that allowed for a lot of shock absorption, and they only required an eleven hundred foot air strip to land on. When we first arrived at Cam Rahn Bay, there was a STOL airfield that seemed like it was in the middle of the bay. One evening while sitting by the railing, I observed some Caribous coming in over our ship using an extremely steep glide path, and engaging in what I would describe as a controlled crash. When the wheels touched the ground, the plane would squat violently down on its landing gear as it came to a rapid stop.

Company-C's commanding officer was Captain Kennedy, and our other officers were a lieutenant and a second lieutenant. There was also a cadre of NCOs ranging in rank from buck sergeant E-5s to First Sergeant Peck who was an E-8. NCOs were section chiefs, supply sergeants, head cooks, etc.; they were the supervisors in charge of making sure

Company C, 725th Maintenance Batallion - Advance Party - First work area at Cu Chi

the privates and specialists were performing their day to day duties in a competent and timely manner. The officers tell the NCOs what they want done, and the NCOs make sure that it gets done. Because we ran the daily supply convoy from Cu Chi into Saigon, our commanding officer had considerable influence over who was getting supplied what and when, especially when it came to items that were in high demand.

Flack jackets were a new item in Vietnam and were in very short supply when we first arrived. These jackets were actually like a thickly padded vest that had straps to keep the front closed (no Velcro yet). We were supposed to wear them every time we went outside Cu Chi's perimeter, but they were hot and heavy. Many soldiers wore them without closing the front opening which left a large part of their body exposed. I recall thinking that I was armor plated when I wore mine, sort of like a security blanket. The reality was that they were only marginal at stopping pistol rounds or shrapnel, and a rifle bullet would barely slow down if it hit your vest. Our support company was among the first to get our flack jackets when they came through the supply chain, but many of the other commanding officers with the infantry and cavalry had to wheel and deal with Captain Kennedy if they wanted their troops to get theirs in a timely manner. I recall thinking that support troops getting their flak jackets before the infantry troops who were actually engaging with the Viet Cong didn't really make too much sense.

During that first month Captain Kennedy along with First Sergeant Peck made another trade that was like no other; they managed to trade for a UH-1 Huey helicopter. Normally Army helicopters are painted olive drab with black markings for insignia and ID,

Repairing small arms under a tarp between the artillery and small arms trucks.
(Note the rifle rack with M-14s in the lower left)(Guy Easton on the right)

but this helicopter was olive drab with absolutely no markings. The unmarked Huey was flown by a warrant officer from the helicopter repair section, and now became Captain Kennedy's personal flying machine so he and First Sergeant Peck could spend their nights in Saigon. This went on for quite a while until some brass up the command chain became aware of what was going on and suddenly the helicopter magically disappeared.

Many officers in Vietnam made an effort to endear themselves with their troops because there was the danger of getting fragged by their own men. Fragging was when troops would murder an officer that they thought was putting his charges in danger by his actions. It could not easily happen with support troops, but was a real danger for officers with fighting troops where his death could be attributed to enemy action. I recall that Captain Kennedy wasn't held in a high regard by many of his troops, and in an effort to help his image and improve troop morale, he scheduled a flag football game between the officers/NCOs and the privates/specialists. When he came out of his hooch to participate in the game, he was wearing a t-shirt with a self-degrading slogan printed on it. He was trying to make us think he was a good guy and a good sport about things, but it all came across as being a little bit phony.

Up until April of 1966 we didn't have much military discipline in our day to day operations. We didn't have to stand formations, we let our hair grow, and we got into a very natural rhythm with our environment. The daily routine became sleeping under our shelter halves, waking up when the sun came up, washing/shaving with hot water placed in our helmet, eating our breakfast rations, working all day with no lunch (our choice), having a beverage at our shelter half after work, eating dinner from a can, and finally going to sleep when

Bombs being dropped north of Cu Chi's perimeter while we worked

the sun went down. During those first months there were always distractions going on that we could observe from inside Cu Chi's perimeter: explosions as the Viet Cong tunnels they had found in the area were blown up, Navy jet fighters on strafing runs with their 20mm cannons, prop driven A1 Skyraiders dropping bombs/napalm, or "Puff the Magic Dragon" (AC47 modified cargo airplane with 3 – 7.62mm Gatling guns) lighting up the night sky with tracers. We also learned to tolerate a battery of M-110 8 inch howitzers firing 200 plus pound shells over our head all night long. As the shells went over our heads, we could actually hear the large projectile as it moved through the air. We became very in tune to the sounds around us and learned to sleep through anything that our brains perceived as normal. However it only took one short round (malfunctioning projectile) from our own artillery or an incoming round and we were up and in our bunker. One evening soon after we first arrived at Cu Chi, the local Viet Cong did manage to lob some mortar rounds at our encampment, but the attack was of very short duration.

My Artillery Repair deuce and a half truck at Cu Chi
(Beyond the treeline in front of my truck was where the heavy infantry and bombing operations were going on)
(The box just to the left of the truck bed contained the bore scope for visually inspecting artillery piece bores.)

Initially we were all scrambling for cover, but when the all clear sounded, we were back preparing to retire to our shelter halves for the night. These small mortar rounds were miniscule when compared to the size and amount of ordnance we were sending in their direction.

We all worked hard during those early days in Vietnam and one of the advantages of being associated with the group running the supply convoys was being able to make trips to Saigon. One day, 6 of us in Company C were selected to go with the daily convoy and spend the night at a hotel in Saigon. First Sergeant Peck gave us the address of a hotel where we should go to make sure we were being treated fairly. We were also instructed to use condoms, wear our civilian clothes, keep out of trouble, and not give any information about our unit to the Vietnamese. As the convoy drove into Saigon, we passed block after block of shanties that were constructed from scrap wood, cardboard, and steel sheeting imprinted with beer logos and signage (rolled steel that hadn't yet been cut to construct beer cans). Most of the refugee peasants that were being driven from the countryside by the war were living in these shanties. On a later trip to Saigon I had occasion to observe many blocks of one of these shanty areas going up in flames; we were driving by at a distance in our convoy and observing the fire racing from shack to shack like we were watching a campfire in our back yard. After passing the shanties, we eventually got to where the permanent structures started and a short while later our

Company C advanced party group at an overnight stay at a hotel in Saigon

trip ended at the supply depot at Long Binh. Those of us that were spending the night at the hotel got a taxi to take us there. In Saigon there were lots of taxis running around like the old Citroen and Peugeot cabs that charged fairly expensive fares. Most of the enlisted men would use peddle cabs for short distances, and for longer trips they used the Lambro scooter-like cabs that had 3 wheels. The Lambros had a rear bed with a bench on either side that ran front to rear, open sides, and a canvas top to protect you from the sun or rain. The passengers in the back sat face to face, and the driver sat up

Here I am checking in at the hotel in Saigon

front in a cab with no doors and he steered the single front wheel with handlebars. As we hopped on a Lambro, we were up for anything and thought we were invincible, but in retrospect these cabs would be pretty dangerous if you were in a crash. After arriving at the hotel, we checked in at the front desk, went to our room, and changed into our civilian clothes. As we checked in I recall being asked to provide information to the desk clerk concerning our unit and job description. We had been told not to divulge this, but First Sergeant Peck had told us which hotel to use, so we all complied with the

Souvenirs from a trip to Saigon

information request. This was the big problem with Vietnam; which locals were friends and which ones were enemies? Which ones were plying you for information during the day and then trying to kill you at night? You just never really knew. We were now off to explore and get something to eat. On every street you walked along in Saigon there were kids and peddlers selling everything: cigarettes, trinkets, their sister, themselves, etc. Black market American cigarettes could be had for 25 cents a pack, and you may ask yourself why anybody would buy cigarettes from a street vendor when you could just buy them for 11 cents from the PX. The answer being that the number of cigarettes a soldier could buy from the PX was rationed, so if you ran out, or didn't have ready access to a PX, where else could you go? After exploring and getting drinks at some bars, we found and settled on a restaurant to eat at. C-rations had been our primary food source for over a month now and hot cooked food was a luxury we were all looking forward to. I ordered a "water buffalo" steak and maybe it was the situation, but I recall that steak as being one of the best I'd ever tasted. I was always much more adventurous than most of my fellow soldiers when it came to food and was willing to try most of the items the local population had to offer. I, however, could never get past the look of the black century eggs (preserved duck eggs) that the Vietnamese considered to be a delicacy. Hotels in Saigon were full service establishments, and if you could pay for something, it was probably available. Around 20:00 that night a mama-san (madam) brought her offerings to the lobby where we selected our partner for the night. Now I assumed that these girls would be willing partners, but many were very young and appeared frightened by their pending sexual experience with an American soldier. My roommate and I made our choices, paid the mama-san the going rate of $4, and headed back to our room. The girls couldn't speak English, so we didn't understand what they were saying to each other when we got them back to our room. The girl that I was with started crying and whimpering, and after a half hour I took her back to the lobby. This probably was not the best thing to do because one of the soldiers still sitting in the lobby piped up that he wanted her. I'm sure the mama-san got paid again and that girl was now on the mama-san's list for not keeping her client happy. The next morning we all got up early, took a cab back to the supply depot, and caught the convoy for the trip back to Cu Chi.

SECURITY COMES FIRST

As the Cu Chi base was being constructed, one of the first things we needed to accomplish was safeguarding our perimeter. The perimeter around the base was miles long and had 10 rows of barbed-wire of various configurations including a 12 foot high woven barbed-wire fence. When the barbed wire was initially set up, they placed trip flares and other devices that were designed to detect persons trying to get through the perimeter. Approximately every two hundred yards we constructed a bunker that had a

| Filling sandbags for our bunker | Bunker where we pulled guard duty |

heavy wooden frame covered with multiple layers of sand bags. The bunkers were 3 to 4 feet thick at their base to shelter its occupants from bullets and shrapnel. Approximately every quarter mile there was a 50 foot tall observation tower that was armored with steel plates and equipped with a .50 caliber machine gun. These towers were manned 24/7 to keep a constant vigil on our perimeter, whereas the ground level bunkers were only manned at night or if we came under attack. Our bunker had an open entrance in the rear protected by sandbag walls, and in the front there were 3 horizontal slits for rifles or machine-guns to fire through. Inside the bunker there was an M-60 machine gun, benches to sit on, and a canvas cot for one person to sleep on. We also had a star scope which was brand new technology that allowed for an intensified image at night using the ambient light available from the moon and stars. In front of the bunker just before the first row of barbed wire, there were 2 Claymore mines (a plastic covered C4 shaped charge that contained 700 small steel balls) that were

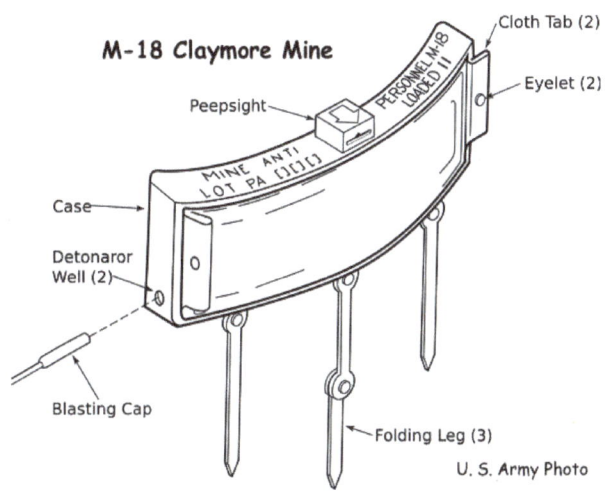

wired into the bunker. In order to fire the Claymore you would connect the wire leads in the bunker to a firing device and then rapidly twist the firing device handle causing an electrical charge to be generated that set off the mine. The Claymore mine had a kill zone of 50 yards in front of the charge and could do damage out to 100 yards. The

Close up of our bunker where we stood guard duty
(We fired an M-60 machine gun and assigned weapons through the horizontal slots to the left. You could fire an M-79 grenade launcher from the protected wall on top.)

bunkers also had a 3-sided sandbag parapet on the top, and we could fire an M-79 grenade launcher or throw hand grenades from that position. It's funny how we had all these weapons at our disposal, but most of us had never actually fired a machine gun or grenade launcher to see how it felt.

When we first got to Cu Chi, anybody in our company that didn't have assigned work to do in their MOS was assigned to sandbag duty and helping with the bunker's construction. Girls from the local villages were eventually hired to fill the sandbags for

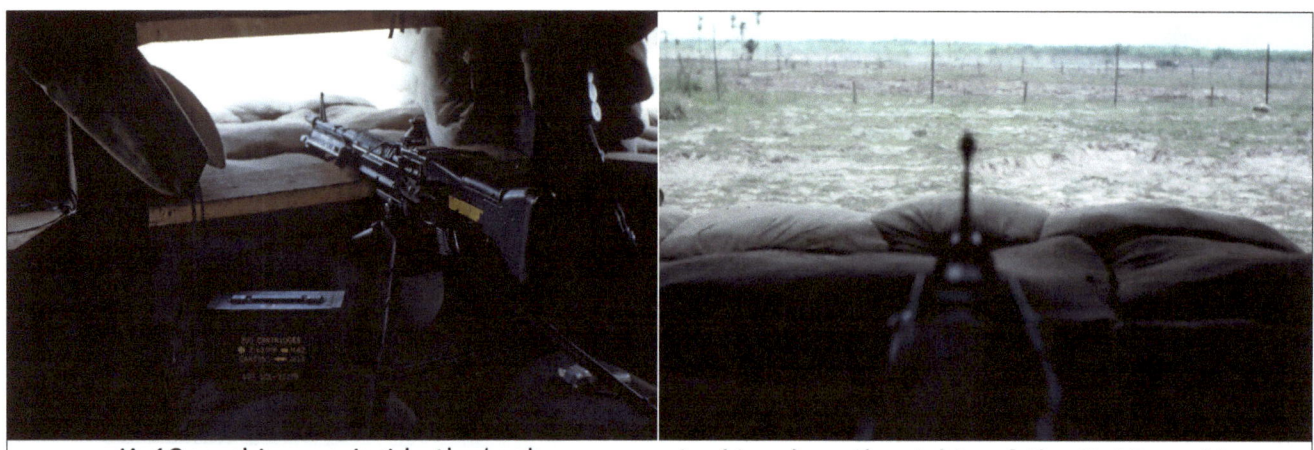

M-60 machine gun inside the bunker
(Black wire on the left for activating the Claymore)

Looking down the sights of the M-60 machine gun

us. They would come through the main gate in the morning, get checked for weapons, and then were escorted to their work area. They were always in groups of 10 to 30 young girls accompanied by an older Vietnamese man (papa-san) who sat around and supervised what his charges were up to. The soldiers and girls would occasionally try to make plans for some extracurricular activities, but there wasn't much opportunity for that and it was mostly idle talk. When it came time for lunch, all the girls would go to a shady area, squat down, and eat whatever they had brought for their noon meal. Sometimes the papa-san would pull out a long pipe and smoke something during the lunch break. SP5 Gauthier, who repaired generators, decided to try the pipe and got violently ill afterwards. We didn't know what was being smoked, but we all suspected it was opium. There was always some idiot soldier who was willing to try anything. After half an hour the girls would get back to work, and when they had finished their day they would be escorted off the base. The girls would fill the sandbags, but we still had to stack them to construct whatever the master plan dictated. We used sandbags for just about everything that needed protection from bullets and shrapnel.

In February of 1966, as I turned 22 years old, I was an old man when compared to most of my peers who were only 18 or 19 years old. Many of them were straight out of high school and had never traveled beyond the area they lived in prior to joining the Army. A great many of them had been drafted, and really didn't want to be in the military. As a result, many of them didn't exercise too much common sense and would get themselves into situations that I considered to be risky. I, on the other hand, had lived in a foreign country, had attended college for two years, and was more reserved and skeptical when it came to new situations that we ran into. I was not looking for trouble or confrontation, and tended to comply with the instructions I was given. I got promoted to SP4 E-4 on February 25th, just after my birthday. In the Army I had always pushed myself to finish first, and making rank before my peers did was high on my list of priorities. I even think the promotion in rank was more important to me than the raise in pay.

Guard duty formation - "Inspection Arms"

Periodically all soldiers were slated for guard duty, and SP4s and below would man the bunkers at night. Initially there were 2 soldiers assigned to each bunker and one could sleep while the other watched the perimeter. Each company at Cu Chi was assigned a section of the perimeter, and they were responsible for staffing guard personnel for that section. When we were picked for guard duty, we would stand formation by our barracks at a selected time and then march to the guard duty area. A portion of the guard detail manned the bunkers, while the rest were assigned to a reactionary force that slept in a large tent located back a few hundred yards from the bunkers on the perimeter. When it came time to post the soldiers assigned to the bunkers, we got in formation, were given our orders for that watch, and then marched to the bunkers to be dropped off where we were assigned. When we got assigned to the reactionary force, we slept with all our clothes and boots on so we were ready to go at a moment's notice. Guard duty at the bunker was always my least favorite job, mainly because you were tasked with guarding the perimeter after having already worked a full day at your normal assignment. Falling asleep while on guard duty was a court marshal offence, but I can tell you it was fairly common for me to doze off while peering through the weapon slits into the dark night. There was no music, talking, or anything to take your mind from the monotonous task. You were praying for daylight to come so you could get back to your regular job and perhaps sneak a nap. When they eventually figured out that soldiers were dozing off, they started assigning 3 soldiers per bunker so 1 could sleep while the other 2 stood guard and kept each other awake.

Being on guard duty always got me thinking because our company's assigned perimeter area was close to Cu Chi's morgue which consisted of a large canvas tent with open sides and tables lined up inside. As we were marching in formation to be dropped of at our bunker, I could often see body bags lying on the tables. It was always a sobering moment that brought home the seriousness of my situation in a hurry.

I was only assigned to the reactionary force one time. At the evening formation we received our orders and instructions before settling into our cots. Whatever the instructions were, I must have not been listening, because I sure had the wrong idea embedded in my brain. We were awakened for a test drill about 02:00, and I immediately grabbed my loaded rifle and made a bee-line for our company's assigned bunker. Now the instructions had been to get up and get into formation to await further orders, but here I was in the dead of night running by myself towards our perimeter bunker. As I approached the bunker, I recall hearing a round being placed into the chamber and a loud voice saying, "Halt or I'll shoot!" At that very instant I realized that I had screwed up badly and immediately stopped in my tracks. Luckily, they didn't fire and after the sergeant had read me the riot act, I was marched back to the reactionary force tent where I slept the rest of the night. In retrospect, what I did by running toward the bunker really didn't make any sense because the Army was always trying to control the chaos. My excitable nature under stress was at the forefront that night, and this incident made me learn to pay more attention to instructions I was given in the future.

Here I am on latrine duty and burning human waste using diesel fuel

Besides guard duty, I was also occasionally selected to perform latrine duty (affectionately called "shit detail"). The containers that were used to hold human waste in the out houses were made from a used 55 gallon drum that had been cut so it had an 18 inch side wall. A container was located under the toilet seat of each stall in the structure that housed 8 to 10 enclosed stalls in a row. Latrine duty involved taking all the containers with waste in them and replacing them with empty ones. Three to four foot long steel rods that had been bent to form a hook on one end and a handle on the other were used to move the drums around so you weren't coming into direct contact with the drums or waste. All the drums containing waste were then pulled to a designated area and stacked for burning. Once they were stacked, diesel fuel was poured on the drums and earth around them, and then set on fire to incinerate the contents. The idea was to burn the full drums today so they would be clean to replace the dirty ones the following day, but many soldiers only did a half-hearted job and left half-burned waste in the drums. Now I, being very conscientious, considered myself to be the best "shit burner" at Cu Chi; I would fan the fires by throwing #10 cans full of diesel on the burning cans to generate an extremely hot fire. I ended up with drums with nothing but gray ash and soot left in them. The thing we all appreciated about latrine duty was that you got some "me time" back at your hooch for the rest of the morning when you'd finished the job.

UH-1 Huey helicopter lifing bales of barbed wire at the Tay Ninh airfield

M-48A3 Tank - Tanks were not that effective around Cu Chi because of the terrain.

View from my truck as we convoy around the Vietnamese countryside

WHAT'S GOING ON HERE?

Each company's commanding officer was allocated funds that were to be used for the entertainment and well being of the troops under his command. While we were still sleeping under our shelter halves and before the rest of the brigade came over in April, they hired a stripper to come dance for all of us. She was a white woman in her late 20s with blonde hair; something that was in very short supply at Cu Chi. When she arrived in one of our company's Jeeps, she and her small entourage were escorted to a round tent on a platform that had been set up for her to spend the night in. Later that evening, she performed her act on a makeshift stage for everyone that wasn't assigned to guard duty, and then retired to her tent for the rest of the evening. All the rest of that night our company's officers were coming and going from her tent where we all assumed further entertainment was being offered. As it turns out, there were a lot of civilian touring groups in the Orient that were approved for entertaining the troops. The commanding officer and first sergeant would simply select from a list and get a booking arranged for a specific date. On another occasion, our company officers and NCOs commandeered some of the tent frame kits and constructed a building featuring a bar for us to spend our evenings in. The soldiers that constructed the bar used a blow torch to accent the wood grain with a burned pattern; that bar was a piece of art. Company C's personal bar and building, just like the personal helicopter, soon disappeared when the misappropriation of the tent frame material was discovered by somebody at the battalion level.

When we first arrived in Vietnam the Red Cross was providing us free cigarettes. Unfortunately our company supply sergeant soon found a way to hijack them and sell them on the black market so he and his cronies could pocket the money. Supply sergeants for the most part could probably make more money selling stuff on the black market than they made in Army pay. I was never invited to participate, but the NCO's would play poker almost every night and there would be 100s of dollars in the pot. Not something a sergeant with a family back in the U.S. could do on his regular pay unless he was making extra money from somewhere. Because we ran the supply convoy into Saigon every day, it was easy to say that something had gotten lost or damaged in shipment, and conversely, persons who were siphoning off supplies had a ready method of getting back into Saigon to sell their merchandise on the black market. At over $100 a case, cigarettes were a lucrative item to sell to a Vietnamese black market entrepreneur, especially when your cost was zero. I think that everyone that was associated with that daily convoy was wheeling and dealing, or at least tempted to develop some scheme to make extra money. One of the schemes used was to purchase beer from the PX in Saigon and then sell the cans for $1 each to the infantry soldiers who had no ready access to such luxuries. The beer would be consumed from the can at temperatures close to 100 degrees because there was no ice. In fact we all got used to drinking canned drinks at warm/hot temperatures. One of my personal favorites was diet Tab at 100 degrees; to this day I still enjoy drinking canned soda at its ambient temperature even if it's been sitting in the sun. The fact that it was wet was more important than the temperature it was consumed at.

When we first set up at Cu Chi, Armament Section had a CONEX container full of captured weapons that had been turned over to us, and we all sort of looked upon this as being our own personal weapons stash. To the best of my knowledge there was no inventory of the container's contents, and no care was taken to limit access within our Armament Section. We had all sorts of weapons that were not part of the Army's normal inventory. Most interesting of which were AK-47s, WWII M-3 grease guns, a hand filed .45 pistol replica, Thompson submachine guns, and 1903 Springfield bolt action rifles. I had occasion to be with the Armament Section's Sergeant Espejo one day when he went on one of his personal missions. He went into the CONEX container and removed a 1903 Springfield 30-06 rifle. From our work area we drove a Jeep to the Cu Chi PX tent where the rifle was exchanged for 4 cases of cigarettes from a soldier who worked there. Souvenir weapons were basically unregulated until 1968, and this rifle was slated to be sent back to the U.S. while the cigarettes had been removed from the PX's inventory and were now destined for the black market. I don't know why I was invited to go along, but it was probably because I was such a straight arrow that many of our company's NCOs were worried that I would report their antics. To assure my silence, I was given a whole case of cigarettes, and thusly I was now complicit in their crimes. I took the case of Salem Menthol 100s and stashed them in every conceivable bit of spare space in the cabinets at the back of my truck. I don't remember how many cartons this was, but for the remainder of my time in Vietnam, I never again had to purchase cigarettes. As my private cigarette stash started running low, they were getting old and stale after having been subjected to the Vietnamese heat and humidity for about 6 months. I was smoking from 2 to 3 packs a day and was actually making myself sick from all the tar and nicotine that my body had to process. It was now that I mentally convinced myself that it was time to quit, and when that last carton was gone, I was through with smoking. I had smoked heavily since I was 13 and now at 22 had just quit "cold turkey". To me it wasn't difficult to quit because I had been constantly coughing and was feeling so physically bad that it was almost a relief to stop torturing myself. After leaving the Army, I took up smoking again and when it later became time to quit at age 40, I simply smoked so much that I got sick and fed up with smoking to accomplish the goal. I have now been smoke free for 30 years.

BACK TO SITUATION NORMAL

One of the most important things that we brought with us from Hawaii was prefab tent frame kits to construct our barracks with when the Army Engineers had finished surveying and building the basic roads and drainage system for the CU Chi base. The kits were composed of pre-cut wood for the frame and plywood for the floors. The wooden

Completed barracks constructed from the tent-frame-kits we brought from Hawaii

walls only went up about 2 feet above the floor with the rest of the frame covered with screening that was stapled to the frame. This framework was covered with a canvas tent with the side flaps held up by poles that were staked to the ground. This allowed the breeze to flow through our sleeping area except during monsoon rains when the flaps were lowered to keep the rain out. Each hooch (barrack) held up to 8 men and their equipment; NCO's and officers each slept in their separate barracks whereas privates and specialists were separated by work area in theirs. Armament Section in my hooch included artillery repairman PFC Wayne Dewberry, small arms repairman SP4 Guy Easton, and fire control instrument repairman SP4 Francisco Ordaz. We all slept on canvas cots and had a plywood footlocker at the foot of our bed; this was a pretty typical Army setup for barracks that started in Basic Training. On one of my trips to Saigon I purchased a two inch thick mattress pad filled with cotton, and I covered it with an olive drab air mattress cover I'd picked up from somewhere. In the year I was in-country I don't recall ever cleaning or changing that cover. Other than the basic cot, anything else you wanted to keep you comfortable was up to you. Because of the heat and humidity, most of us slept with no cover/sheet and simply wore our olive drab boxer shorts.

Both Guy and Francisco were drafted and had a different perspective regarding the Army than I did. I had a hard time understanding Francisco's situation because he lived in El Paso, but he had been drafted as a non U.S. citizen. He told me his choice had been get drafted into the Army or leave his family and go back to Mexico. Additionally, he informed me that even after he had completed his military service there was no guarantee of U.S. Citizenship for him. In my liberal haze at that time, I didn't consider his situation to be very fair. Francisco was a reluctant soldier at best.

Here's me working on a carpentry project during the monsoon season

The construction of our barracks was supervised by officers and NCOs who had been trained in Hawaii before we left. Most of us were relegated to maintaining the equipment that our MOS dictated, but anyone that didn't have maintenance duties was sent to work on either bunker building or tent frame construction. SP4 Harvey Young, who was with the Armament Section, was assigned to tent frame construction because he was trained to repair French ENTAC wire guided anti-tank missiles, and there weren't any ENTACs at Cu Chi. While I was in Vietnam, Harvey never had any work in his assigned MOS and was always floating around working in areas that needed help. After hanging out with and brown nosing with the company NCOs at every opportunity, he eventually got promoted to buck sergeant (E-5) working in supply before I left to go home. They were in a hurry to get the barracks finished before the monsoon season so we wouldn't be sleeping on the ground, but they missed that deadline by about a week. I can remember viewing with awe the power of the storm clouds boiling out of Cambodia. Whenever a storm hit we were presented with driving rain that came at us vertically. The first storm was so severe that it lifted two of the newly constructed barracks off their concrete base piers. After that they learned how to stake them down so they wouldn't fly.

Generator repair during the monsoon
(Note the smoke in the background from military operations)

Vehicle boneyard near our early work area
(Jeep driver didn't realize how deep the monsoon puddle was)

When the barracks were finished, the Army hired locals to place and monitor rat traps under them. When a rat got trapped, the Vietnamese would start talking excitedly as they recovered their prize. Around camp it was said that the Vietnamese ate the rats and considered them a delicacy. I could never quite believe this, but upon returning to the States I saw a picture taken in Cambodia that was captioned "Harvest Festival." In

Sitting in front of my hooch   Looking out across Company C's barracks

the picture was a pile of dressed rats that were slated to be deep fried by dropping them into a large round black pot full of hot oil. I can now assume that if you ate the local faire; you really didn't know what was in the meal.

Here is a situation that most civilians will find hard to understand! Here we are in a war zone with our assigned rifles and taking mortar fire, but there is no ammunition in our weapon. Whenever we were in base camp or a situation where having access to a loaded weapon could be more dangerous to our fellow soldiers than the enemy, the Army would simply not give you ready access to ammunition. The logic being that firing your assigned weapon in an uncontrolled or indiscriminate manner inside the base camp was very likely going to result in harm to one of your fellow soldiers. Firing at something outside the perimeter was fair game, but what happened inside the perimeter had to be strictly controlled. We always had our rifle with us, except when we were in our sleeping area or were going on some type of R&R. While we were in our sleeping area our rifles were kept propped up on a welded metal rack just inside the entrance door. I can tell you one thing however, no matter where we were, we always knew where to get ammunition from. There are a lot of things that go on in the military that don't make much sense until you really think them through.

In April of 1966 the rest of the brigade began arriving from Hawaii. As an advanced party we had grown used to a lack of military discipline and with the arrival of more troops came the realization that we were going to be returning to normal military formations and routines. We had slept under the stars in our shelter halves, lived off C-rations, grown our hair long, and built the housing and basic conveniences that the arriving troops would benefit from. We had become a very cohesive unit and were having fun while we did it. Here the new arrivals were getting flown in by helicopter and then being ushered into a large tent where they were greeted by the Red Cross Donut Dollies

Lightning strike at Cu Chi

and served punch. All us Cu Chi veterans laughed and looked on this as being a joke. We all commented on what a bunch of pussies these guys were. As I stated earlier, making rank was personally important to me because I deemed this as a validation of my having done a good job. Back at AIT in Aberdeen the soldier who had graduated 2nd in our class was assigned to Headquarters & Company A of the 725th Maintenance Battalion. My fellow classmate had arrived by helicopter and a couple months later he was promoted to SP5, E-5. Now this was almost more than I could stand as I was one "gung ho" soldier and I felt I had gone above and beyond under very trying conditions. Here this guy was getting the easy entrance to Vietnam and then getting the promotion I thought I was due. I started complaining to my fellow soldiers and threatening to go to the inspector general. Of course Captain Kennedy and First Sergeant McCloskey looked upon my actions as affecting troop morale. Before long, I was called in for a meeting of the minds and threatened with court marshal if I didn't stop. I can recall being totally frustrated and had to fight back tears before I reluctantly agreed to stop. However, they did offer me the promotion if I would extend my tour of duty by 6 months. Up to this point I had been very enthusiastic about Army life, but from this point on I made up my mind that extending my tour or reenlisting was not for me. I would do my job, but just like most of the troops around me, only perform in a manner required to keep me from getting into trouble.

WORK ASSIGNMENT CU CHI

Our Company C work area moved several times as the Cu Chi Base Camp was being constructed. Our section sergeant would lead us to our new assigned work area, and we

Two of the armament section's early work areas at Cu Chi
(The engineers eventually developed a decent drainage system and the muddy work areas became less frequent)

would line up the Armament Section (small arms, artillery, and fire control) trucks, hang our signs on the back of our truck, and wait for business to come our way. I was responsible for maintenance at the direct support level to the 1/8th and 2/23rd Artillery Battalions. This involved four M-110 8 inch howitzers, four M-107 175mm cannons and over 100 M-101A1 towed 105mm howitzers. Eight inch howitzers and 175mm cannons were on a tracked, self-propelled chassis and were the big weapons in the Army's inventory. Eight inch howitzers fired a 200+ pound projectile up to 16 miles while a 175mm cannon was capable of tossing a 147 pound projectile up to 20 miles down range. In both of these weapons the projectile is separate from the powder charge. The smaller 105mm howitzers were either towed behind a vehicle or transported underneath CH-47 twin-rotor helicopters. The 105mm projectile and powder are contained in a large casing that looks like a large rifle cartridge; the big difference is that it's 4.1 inches in diameter.

I also provided maintenance for the infantry's heavy weapons, the M-30 107mm "4 Deuce" and M-29 81mm mortars as well as 90mm and 105mm recoilless rifles. The 81mm mortar and 90mm recoilless rifle were used at the company level whereas the "4 Deuce"

Checking out a towed 105mm howitzer   M-107 175mm self propelled gun

Artillery encampment with 105 howitzers and OH-13 observation helicopters

25th Division Artillery supports infantry operations near the Ho Bo Woods northwest of Cu Chi

mortar provided heavy support at the battalion level. The 81mm mortar had a range of 5,000 yards, normally required a team of 5 soldiers, and could be hand carried for short distances. The "4 Deuce" was the infantry's big weapon, and because it weighed over 600 pounds with its base plate it was often mounted in an APC (armored personal carrier). All the "4 Deuce" mortars I ran across were ground mounted, and I can imagine it was quite a chore to carry one around in a truck or Jeep and then set it up just using manpower. Mortars were very reliable and rarely required maintenance because they had minimal moving parts. The 90mm and 105mm recoilless rifles were more problematic however, and I was always getting complaints about reliability from the soldiers that used them. The 90mm was held on the shoulder like a bazooka, whereas the 105mm was Jeep mounted. Recoilless rifles are used for direct fire missions and use a large shell just like a 105mm howitzer. The difference being that the shell has vent holes in the cartridge and the

Infantry four deuce mortor encampment during field operations near Cu Chi
(This is one place where I got stuck overnight and slept on ammo tubes to keep off the damp ground)

Airlifting a 105mm howitzer with a CH-47 helicopter during field operations near Cu Chi

breach of the rifle has open sections to allow some of the burning gunpowder to escape to the rear as the projectile is pushed down the barrel. This allows for a light weight, large caliber weapon with no recoil because as much force escapes to the rear as there is pushing the projectile forward in the barrel. The downside is that the projectile has a much lower muzzle velocity than a conventional gun, and it was extremely noisy. The gasses escaping behind the weapon could also make it dangerous to personnel and equipment if they were behind it. The one time I observed one in the field, the force of the blast flattened small trees that were behind the weapon.

Large artillery pieces in the Army are required to have a log book, and one of my primary jobs as a direct support specialist was to periodically inspect these weapons and certify that they were safe to operate. I used a weapon specific bore gauge to assure that the bore diameter was within tolerances. Visual inspection for abnormal wear patterns or defects inside the guns and howitzers was accomplished with a bore scope which is a series of long thin interlocking tubes that has optics at one end and a mirror/prism with a light source at the other end. The bore scope was stored on my truck in a wooden storage box that was 10 to 12 feet long. Assembling the scope involved locking together the appropriate number of tubular sections needed for the weapon's barrel length and then placing bore diameter ring adapters on the long tube to center the tube in the bore. I now shoved the assembled scope into the muzzle end of the weapon and connected it to

Cu Chi Base helicopter airstrip area | UH-1 helicopter lifting off

Deuce and a half truck stuck up to its frame in mud
(The M-113 APC pulled it out like it was nothing)

an electrical source to turn on the light. Periodically, my particular bore scope would short and shock me when I moved it, but inspecting the weapon had to be completed anyway. With the scope shoved down into the combustion chamber, I would rotate the scope through 360 degrees to observe the barrel's interior condition. Then the scope was pulled back up the barrel about 6 inches and again rotated through 360 degrees to observe the next section of the barrel's interior. This procedure was repeated until the entire length of the weapons barrel had been inspected. I can tell you that this got very tedious and time consuming on a 175mm cannon that had a 34.5 foot barrel; in addition I had to work from a step ladder on the 8 inch and 175mm weapons in order to look down the scope. I was trying to compare what I was seeing with pictures that I had seen in advanced training and hoping I didn't screw up. At the end of the inspection I got to sign

Company C on field operations near Cu Chi   Artillery encampment with 105 howitzer

Infantry soldiers returning to the Cu Chi Base Camp after field operations

off in the weapon's log book and certify that everything was safe to operate until the next inspection came due. The time interval till the next inspection was determined by the number of rounds through the barrel or if something abnormal occurred. The artillery officer in charge of the weapon was responsible for scheduling the next inspection when it came due.

At the end of my one year tour, we were exchanging gun barrels on some of the 105mm howitzers because they had 100,000 rounds (end of life) through them. Now I don't think all these rounds were fired in Vietnam because the 105mm howitzers were WWII/Korean War vintage, but in any case this was a lot of 4.1 inch diameter, 33 pound projectiles to be throwing up to 7 miles down range. We would swap out the 1200 pound barrels by hand and it took 10 to 12 men plus me directing to accomplish this. We used teams of 2 with 3 foot 2X4's to support the old barrel as we slid it out of the artillery piece. After placing the old barrel on the ground, the pairs of men would lift the new barrel from its wooden shipping crate and I would guide it into place. After securing the new barrel with its retaining ring and reassembling the breach mechanism, the weapon was returned to service.

In Vietnam there just wasn't enough time, and I often didn't have enough patience to accomplish some jobs like we were trained in school. The extreme dust in Vietnam was forcing us to replace the brass bushings on the 105mm howitzer's towing eye attachment. My training in AIT involved special tools and a time consuming fitting process using fine grit crocus cloth. The reality in the field was using a hammer with a piece of 2X4 to soften the blows and sand paper. Differences in the individual weapons sometimes made getting the new bushing to fit properly very difficult, and one time I had to use 3 new bushings because I had damaged the first 2 with my hammering. That particular howitzer absolutely ate my lunch, and when I had finished the job I was wondering if the new bushing was much better than the original one. The expression we all used at this point was, "Close enough for government work." I was then off to the next job.

Guy Easton repaired small arms in the truck on one side of mine, and Francisco Ordaz repaired fire control instruments in the truck on the other side. Problems with the early M-16s kept Guy quite busy for a while because some of the plastic parts on the new rifle were deteriorating in the heat and humidity of Vietnam and needed to be replaced. On his truck, Guy had one thing that a lot of the infantry soldiers thought they wanted: a drawer full of M-16 selector switches. A standard issue M-16 only fired in semi-automatic mode; one round fired for every pull of the trigger. With a selector switch installed you could choose between semi-automatic or automatic mode by turning a lever located on the right side of the weapon ¼ turn. In automatic mode the rifle kept firing as long as you held down on the trigger. This of course went through a lot of ammunition, and an uninitiated soldier could overheat and damage the rifle's barrel. Normally your commanding officer had to sign off on having a selector switch installed, but Guy would use installing a selector switch on the infantryman's M-16 as a bargaining chip in return for war souvenirs. A lot of what went on at Cu Chi in early 1966 depended on what you had to bargain with. If it was a want, and not a critical need, it was fair game. Artillery parts had no value in the trading market which left me few options when it came to bartering.

When we first got to Cu Chi, Guy spent a lot of time repairing M-2 .50 caliber machine guns but one of the big problems was where to test fire them. We eventually got permission to construct a pit to test fire weapons into. The Army engineers dug a sloping trench with a bulldozer so we could fire into an earthen wall. The trench was approximately 100 feet long by 12 feet wide and sloped down to 8 feet deep with a vertical wall of earth at the end. Over the deep end of the pit we laid logs covered with sandbags to capture ricochets if they occurred. The pit was situated where no troops were in the direction the weapons were being fired at, but we were inside the perimeter and we had to be careful that no bullets got above the pit. The machine guns were placed on a tripod set up at the shallow end of the pit, and we were soon firing at #10 cans filled with water. The steel jacketed .50 caliber bullets would pass completely through the cans and simply poke a hole in them. This was no fun, so in our infinite wisdom we decided to take some bullets and cross cut notches in the bullet tips with a hack saw. Now we were into something because the cans of water would literally explode when they were hit; this was great fun. I'm sure, however, that there was some officer who wouldn't have been too happy to discover we were making dum-dum bullets in complete disregard of the Geneva Convention. I can recall another time when Guy was test firing an M1911 .45 pistol that had detent problems. When he pulled the trigger, the pistol fired continuously until the magazine was empty. He wasn't able to control the recoil, and every time the pistol fired it was aiming a little bit higher. The last bullet went above the sandbags at the end and we were really sweating this one. Fortunately no one was hit and after this we learned to only put a couple rounds in .45 pistol clips when we test fired them. The pit was eventually filled in because some officer was afraid the logs with the sand bags on top would rot and collapse on someone who was under them.

Changing out a track link on our M-88 tank recovery vehicle
(This tracked vehicle was used like a heavy duty wrecker and its crane was used to lift heavy equipment)

Medical air evacuation during field operations near Cu Chi
(I was with CWO Pinkney at the time and he was urging me to get some close ups - I declined to interfere)

Do not park your loaded diesel fuel tanker too close to the shoulder of the road
(This picture was taken from the cab of my artillery repair truck)
(Across the street are the APCs and tanks of the 3rd Squadron of the 4th Cavalry)(POW detainment area in upper right)

Aerial view of the jungle terrain near Cu Chi showing the pock marked landscape

Aerial view looking west of Cu Chi towards the Cambodian border
(Note the brown paths of dead vegetation where agent orange had been aerially sprayed to defoliate the jungle)

My truck had a canvas top on the bed, but Francisco's fire control repair truck had a completely enclosed bed because he had to clean optical sights and required dust free conditions. I know that with the heat and humidity of Vietnam, it was terribly hot when I had to work under the canvas cover on the back of my truck. I, at least, had the option of rolling up the canvas sides to allow the breezes to flow through. Francisco had no such options. I don't remember if Francisco's truck had air conditioning, but it would have been unbearable work conditions if he didn't. His was also a lonely occupation as he was forced to work by himself within a confined space when he was cleaning or calibrating his delicate instruments. Artillery and small arms got to work outside most of the time and we often conversed with each other as we worked.

Small arms and fire-control always repaired their equipment in their trucks back at base, but most of my work had to be done at the place where the weapon was at. I spent a lot of time traveling in a Jeep throughout the base camp performing my duties, but occasionally I had to travel beyond the barbed wire by Jeep or helicopter to where the sick howitzer or mortar was located at. Our M-14 rifles were fairly heavy at 11 pounds when fully loaded, and I also had to carry my tools when I went to repair artillery away from our shop area. For some unexplained reason I became enamored with a captured grease gun and started carrying that when I traveled. The M-3 grease gun was a stamped steel submachine gun that had been developed during WWII for paratroopers and tank troops. It had a 30 round magazine, and fired .45 caliber pistol ammunition. This would have been

accurate up to about 50 yards, but because it only fired automatically, you could go through 30 rounds very rapidly. Here I was, just barely qualified with an M-14, carrying a WWII weapon that I had never fired, and thus didn't know if it even worked. Any sane soldier would have been using their familiar standard issue weapon, but I must have been going for the dramatic so that artillery or infantry soldiers I was visiting would be impressed. The standard inquiry I got was, "What's that?" After we had been in-country a couple of months, the infantry troops began getting M-16s to replace their M-14s. They eventually got around to replacing our M-14s as well and at that point I was glad to give up my grease gun.

On my first maintenance trips outside Cu Chi's perimeter I carried my standard issue metal toolbox with me. The toolbox was unwieldy to carry, so I found a metal framed rucksack that I packed with the tools I needed to repair artillery pieces in the field. The full rucksack probably weighed about 60 pounds, but was much easier to get around with than the tool box. I was in pretty good shape at this time, and once had to run with that heavy rucksack on my back for about a half mile so I could catch a helicopter back to base camp. I would normally travel by helicopter to the customer's site, perform my duties, and then catch a helicopter back to base. The helicopter was usually the workhorse UH-1 "Huey" that Vietnam made famous, but on one occasion I got a ride back in an observation helicopter OH-13. The OH-13 had an open tubular frame, and a globe like glass enclosure that the pilot and passengers sat in. The pilot sat in the middle and there was a seat on either side where passengers could sit. As a passenger it felt like one ass-cheek was on the seat and the rest of your ass was hanging out in space. You had to put a lot of faith in your lap belt that strapped you in. The "Huey" flew fast and high, but observation helicopters flew low and slow. The idea was to skim about 50 feet over the tree tops so if you came across any Viet Cong in the jungle below, your time exposure to any enemy fire was minimal. On this one trip we did manage to take some fire on our way back to base, but luckily no damage was done. On another maintenance trip I got to travel in a CH-47 back to base. This was completely different from flying in a single rotor helicopter because with twin rotors the front of the aircraft would act independently from the rear making it very hard to get your bearings. The experienced soldiers on board said it was common for CH-47 initiates to get motion sick.

On a couple occasions I got stuck in the field and had to spend the night under very uncomfortable conditions. One time after repairing a "4 Deuce" there was no helicopter to get me back to base, and I ended up sleeping in the open on top of cardboard ammunition tubes that had been laid on the ground. Being unable to get back to base and having no shelter to sleep under was never any fun. I would go to almost any length to avoid the experience, but on one occasion I was working on an infantry 81mm mortar when the platoon leader, a second lieutenant, became convinced that I needed to experience being an infantryman. Not only did he not call for a helicopter, but he assigned me to guard duty on their encampment's perimeter. This was not like being in a fortified bunker at base camp. There was only an open shallow trench with a few sandbags in front of us for protection if we came under fire. From our slightly elevated position we could see, in our star scope's green tinged view, some rice paddies with thatch-roofed farm homes and buildings off to the left. Back at base camp we were never allowed to fire our weapons when we were on guard duty unless we were damn sure something was coming through the barbed wire. These infantry soldiers were firing their M-16's throughout the night because they thought they saw something move. They kept letting me look through the star scope, but I could never see anything move. Hopefully they had informed the locals not to be moving around at night, because I got the impression that these soldiers didn't know or care about what they were firing at. I also don't recall anyone being overly concerned that there were rifles being fired. Maybe this was all part of my infantryman's training? This proved to be the only time I was involved in a situation where rifles were being fired at the enemy, and to me there was some doubt if the enemy was even there.

Whenever we left the base camp in a group we always traveled in a convoy, and on a few occasions we were called on to support a major war operation away from base camp. Whenever this happened we were again relegated to sleeping under our shelter halves. In the fall of 1966 we were involved with a major 2nd Brigade operation and Company C moved by convoy to Tay Ninh which is 40 miles northwest of Cu Chi. As we slowly drove towards our destination, I was looking around at the fertile, lush, green countryside, and

Here's my truck lined up and ready for the convoy trip to Tay Ninh

Storage area at Tay Ninh airfield with Black Virgin Mountain in the background

thinking what a shame it was that there had to be a war going on. Road conditions on the dirt road were fairly good, but we really slowed to a crawl when we came to sections that had been blown up by the Viet Cong. One of those damaged sections was almost 100 yards across by 8 feet deep, and the Army engineers had built a detour into the field next to the crater to get around the problem. The MPs were directing us to the detour, and to get through I had to put my truck into low range, all wheel drive. We finally arrived at Tay Ninh, and set up in an area next to the airfield. Off to one side of our bivouac area there was a storage area surrounded by coiled barbed-wire and with pallet-load after pallet-load of supplies left in the open. We were again living off C-rations, so some of my fellow soldiers decided to go see what items of interest were in the storage area. The coiled barbed wire was of little deterrent and they soon came back with several items of interest. The one item most of us really enjoyed was freeze dried food pouches that were designed for long range patrols. Reconstituting the food involved opening the olive drab foil pouch, pouring in some hot water, rolling the top of the pouch back up, and letting it sit for a couple minutes. The end result was a hot meal that was almost like something prepared in a kitchen. Rice, beef, and vegetables or the like; it was all good. In the evening, after working all day, we would often sit on our locally procured flimsy aluminum framed beach chairs and enjoy a tasty beverage or two before going to

Results of a Jeep hitting a roadside mine close to Tay Ninh
(The airfield landing strip is the paved area in the background on the left picture)

48

On the way to the Tay Ninh airfield with Black Virgin Mountain rising from the plain

sleep. One evening we were lounging around before it got dark when we started hearing explosions coming from across the airfield's runway. A quarter mile away on the other side of the landing strip it was total chaos; we could see soldiers running everywhere seeking shelter because they were undergoing a mortar attack. On our side of the airstrip we just continued sitting in our chairs, drinking our beverages, viewing what was going on like it was a movie, and commenting on how we were glad we weren't on their side of the field. Vietnam was full of many situations that sometimes seemed too improbable to believe. On a different day Lieutenant Lewis had me drive him to an area close by our

Here I am at Tay Ninh standing by a 105mm howitzer just as the sun is going down
(The howitzer had just been dropped from a helicopter and you can see the bent steel frame)

encampment to see the results of a Jeep that had run into a roadside mine. The driver had been killed, and the vehicle was a tangled mess with the whole left front of the vehicle just missing.

Jet fighter at Tan Son Nhat Airfield, SaigonAir Force C-123 cargo airplane U. S. Air Force Photo

In my travels around Vietnam, I got to fly in an Air Force C-123 fixed wing aircraft a couple of times. The C-123s were built by Fairchild, had 2 piston driven radial engines, and because of their ability to use short air strips, they were the Air Force's answer to the Army's Caribou. With their 60 passenger capacity, C-123s were larger than the Caribou, and were used all over Vietnam to transport supplies as well as spraying Agent Orange defoliant. The Cu Chi map in this book shows an airstrip for C-123s, but this hadn't been built yet when I was there, so I must have been flying out of the airstrip at Tay Ninh. I liked flying in the C-123 because after take off you could unbuckle, stand at the cockpit door, observe what was going on in the cockpit, and view through the front windshield. Airplanes in Vietnam always used an extremely steep glide path to avoid ground fire when coming into landing strips. On one of my C-123 flights, we were approaching Tan Son Nhat Airfield in Saigon and descending rapidly on final approach. Suddenly the pilot started cursing, pushed forward on the throttles, and manipulated the plane's controls to abort the landing. As our plane slowed its descent, I observed 2 F-4 Phantom fighters in front of us on the runway. With their afterburners at full burn, they had just been starting their take off, and without the C-123 pilot's quick thinking and actions we probably would have landed on top of them. That is as close as I ever want to be when it comes to experiencing a plane crash.

The first part of October at Cu Chi soon after dark, some of us were in front of our hooch drinking a beer and enjoying the evening air. I was looking to the south-east towards Saigon when a huge mushroom cloud rose up in the distance. A short time later we heard the explosion and we all knew something big had blown up close to Saigon. This was the middle of the Cold War and some soldiers speculated that someone had set off a nuclear device in Saigon. There was no call to arms from our command so we all went to bed that night wondering what had happened. The next day we learned that the Viet Cong had gotten into the ammo storage at Long Binh, which was one of the largest storage depots in Vietnam, and blown up a portion of it. When you realize that Long Binh is 25 miles from Cu Chi, you will understand how large an explosion this was for us to be able to observe and hear it. I, for one, was gratified that Vietnam wasn't going nuclear.

R&R AND OTHER FUN ACTIVITIES

Many of us soldiers in Vietnam were into photography, and as a teenager I had learned photography from my dad using the darkroom equipment that he had in his younger years. I had always done black & white photography and my cameras had been inexpensive Kodak Brownies or the like. As a young child I recall going to the Rexall Drug Store in Dixfield, Maine and buying my first Brownie for $2. When we were back in Hawaii, I had purchased an inexpensive 35mm camera from the PX. This was a good starter camera, but once they got the PX set up at Cu Chi I started to think bigger and better. A 35mm Nikon with an f-1.2 lens was over $100 and more than I wanted or could afford to pay, but we all craved that Nikon f-1.2 lens. We all wanted that low f-stop on the camera lens so you could take low light photos without a flash. Using flash bulbs in a war zone might draw unwanted attention to your position. I finally settled on a Canon 35mm SLR with an f-1.6 lens for around $60. The price included the camera body, lens, and a fitted leather case with carrying strap. This Canon had absolutely no automatic features. The film advancement, f-setting, lens focus, and shutter speed all had to be manually set before taking the picture and I had no light meter to help me with the settings. If you forgot to advance the film you would double expose the picture and end up with a wasted shot. I probably wasted quite a few pictures when I first started, but soon learned to take some pretty good pictures by just using my knowledge of the available light and what the situation required for settings. I took this camera with me everywhere and tried to record everything that I came into contact with. There were some situations I got into where picture taking was the last thing on my mind, but I did manage to take hundreds of pictures during my year in Vietnam. I would purchase prepaid Kodak film mailers from the PX, take pictures with the roll of film, and then drop it off in the mail to Kodak. I don't remember how much the mailers cost, but it couldn't have been very much because I bought lots of mailers. In a couple weeks the developed prints or slides would come back for all of us to view. I started taking a lot of slides using Ektachrome or Kodachrome film, and bought a portable, single slide at a time projector from the PX. The Kodachrome had an ASA film speed of 25; not too good for low light, but great for high resolution. Many years later, 2011 and 2013, two of these slide pictures would be selected for use in the annual calendar of the 25th Infantry Division Association. Before I left Vietnam I sold my Canon to another soldier and bought a Miranda 35mm SLR that had a light meter and motor drive for film advancement built into the camera.

Starting in 1966, the military flew 3 converted TWA Super Constellation prop airplanes and broadcasted a TV signal from one of the planes as it circled at 15,000 to 18,000 feet above Saigon. They initially just broadcast news from 20:00 to 23:00, but soon expanded their broadcast hours and added many popular TV shows from back home to their offerings. Black and white TV sets were available at the PX and the soldier living in the bunk across from me had a 12-inch portable we all watched after work. Our favorite program was "Batman" with all its crazy antics, and I recall everyone hurrying back to our hooch when it was on so we could watch. Wayne Dewberry used to act out the scenes from the show and had us all laughing.

Some of the soldiers at Cu Chi would get pets and keep them at their hooches. I don't recall anyone having a cat or dog, but many went for more exotic animals like monkeys. The soldiers would purchase the monkeys from the local market and take them back to camp. In all my travels in the forests surrounding Cu Chi, I never saw a monkey in the wild. That led me to believe that they must have been imported from another region of Vietnam. Most of the monkeys were Macaques and they needed to be chained in order to keep them under control. A loose monkey in camp could have done a lot of damage and been very difficult to recapture. The monkey's owner often wouldn't be around and other soldiers walking by would tease them to watch and laugh at their reaction. These monkeys didn't really make good pets because they tended to get quite mean after being chained up all the time.

Chained Up Monkey

During a one year tour in Vietnam everyone was entitled to one 2 day in-country R&R (rest and recuperation) and one 6 day out-of-country R&R. When we were on R&R, or off base and not conducting Army business, we were required to wear civilian clothing. On R&R the army paid for your transportation, but you had to prearrange your accommodations and pay for your own meals and entertainment. This meant a soldier had to save up money for this, and some soldiers seemed incapable of saving any amount of money. Their plea was always, "lend me twenty and I'll pay you thirty on pay day." They were always borrowing money and waiting for the next pay day to pay it back; a week after payday they would be back in the same rut and borrowing money again. The military didn't pay us in U.S. dollars while in-country, but we got paid in military script (the military printed their own money) which had U.S. dollar equivalent value. You could use it on base and at the PX, but weren't supposed to use it with the civilian population. The reason the military used script was because it only had value in Vietnam, and the enemy wasn't able to use captured funds to purchase items on the world market. We were supposed to exchange our money for Dong (Vietnamese money) when we went off base, but of course the resourceful Vietnamese civilians would take Dong or script to get your business. Genuine U.S. money was worth a lot on the on the black market, but a court marshal was in your future if you got caught having real money in your possession. Now let's get back to the R&R situation. The destinations for an out-of-country R&R were Hong Kong, Sydney, Bangkok, Kuala Lumpur, and if you were married, Hawaii. The Army had a long list of dos and don'ts, but one was pretty much left up to their own devices once they arrived at their destination,

When it came time for my out-of-country R&R, I decided to go to Hong Kong. I had 60 dollars saved up, which in 1966 would go a long way anywhere in the Orient. I got teamed up with another SP4 from Company C, and we made our reservations at an approved hotel in Kowloon (the inexpensive section of Hong Kong). On our departure day we made our way to the R&R Departure Center at Tan Son Nhat Airfield in Saigon where we received information about Hong Kong and exchanged our military script for Hong Kong dollars. The exchange rate was about 5.7 for 1, so having $60 U.S. in Hong Kong was almost like having $350 back in the States. We finally boarded a Pan American DC-6 (4 engine prop plane) full of GIs and were off for the 950 mile flight across the South China Sea. The flight seemed long, but we were glad to be away from Vietnam even if it was only going to be for 6 days.

After arriving at Hong Kong, my buddy and I finally made it to the hotel where we checked in. We were young, impatient, and ready for some action, so we immediately were on the go looking for trouble: bars, drinks, and women. We managed to find two willing females and brought them back to our hotel. We walked past the hotel's front desk under the disapproving stares of the hotel's clerk and went up to our room. Being neophytes to R&R protocol, the women left soon after, and we both discovered the next morning that almost all our money was gone. Here we were only on our second day and already facing a dire situation. Thankfully we had prepaid for our room, but there was still the matter of food, transportation, and fun for the remainder of our vacation. In Cu Chi there wasn't much to spend money on, so thankfully I had the Army sending a portion of every pay check to my dad to put into a savings account. All it would take was a call to my dad so he could wire me some money from my savings account, but operator assisted, person to person, international phone calls were $4.80 U.S. per minute. With 12 hours time difference to Massachusetts, I calculated a good time to call my dad, and then traveled to the Hong Kong phone company office. Once there I had to fill out a form, prepay the call, and then wait for the operator to make the call and page me to the phone. Needless to say, that phone call was short and to the point. My dad wired me the $60 and with that I was able to buy some custom tailored suits, find a new girl friend, eat many varieties of Chinese cuisine, buy some gifts to send home, and see many of the sights that Hong Kong had to offer.

An approved merchant area was inside the U.S. Naval Station on Hong Kong Island, but getting there involved taking a ferry from Kowloon to Hong Kong Island. We had been advised to order suits from the Navy merchant area, but I was looking for the quick easy way and succumbed to the sales pitch of some tailor that was close to our hotel. Form fitting suits were all the fashion rage back then, so of course my suits were custom fitted to my body. I wasn't taking into consideration the fact that I had become fit and trim from working in the heat and humidity of Vietnam, and with the short duration of my vacation I wouldn't have much time to correct any problems with the tailoring. After my final fitting, I recall commenting how tight the fit was on the suits, but the time to return to Vietnam and the realities of the war was at hand, so I took the suits like they were. When I eventually got back to the States where I could wear my suits, I was never able to fit into them and there wasn't enough spare material to alter them. They hung in my clothes closet for many years before I finally gave up on ever being able to fit into them.

Vung Tau, where we first set foot on Vietnamese soil, was not only by the entrance to the Saigon River, but it was also an old colonial French resort on the South China Sea. Vung Tau was the designated in-country R&R center for all the soldiers around Saigon, and had miles of beautiful white sand beaches as well as offering any vice that a soldier could possibly want to indulge in. The U.S. military ran an R&R Center at Vung Tau, but reservation space was limited, and a soldier was restricted regarding what type of activities he could conduct inside the facility. Vietnamese and U.S. Army MPs (Military Police) were everywhere in the city, and we were led to believe that the whole area around Vung Tau was fairly safe. There was even talk amongst us soldiers that the Viet Cong sent their soldiers there for rest as well. The truth of the matter was that Viet Cong spies probably ran rampant in the city. In Saigon, it was not uncommon for someone to lob a grenade inside bars that were popular with U.S. soldiers, but I never heard of this happening at Vung Tau. No matter where you were in Vietnam, you were warned to be aware of your situation and be prepared for anything.

Sex was for sale everywhere in Vietnam, especially at in-country R&R areas, and nobody was asking how old any of these girls were. The word was that many refuge families were selling their very young daughters to pimps and madams in order for the rest of the family to survive. These young girls would work in some mama-san's housing establishment observing, learning, cleaning and doing other menial chores until their time came to start earning money as a prostitute for the mama-san; it was sort of like an apprenticeship. In Vung Tau, the MPs would periodically go on a sweep of all the prostitutes they could find and take them to the Army's medical staff to be checked and treated for STDs. The prostitutes would always complain about and try to avoid these medical sweeps, but it became a tolerated part of their existence. The price for a prostitute procured through an established mama-san was around $4 a night in places like Saigon and Vung Tau, but sex could be had for much less from street walkers and girls in the countryside if a participant and place could be found. One street prostitute I ran into was the wife of a Vietnamese soldier who was supplementing her family's income. On my first R&R to Vung Tau my buddy and I decided to try a bar that was frequented by officers and NCOs that had money to burn. All the women in the bar were absolutely gorgeous, but the $25 per night price tag was too rich for our wallets.

When I was on my scheduled 2 day in-country R&R at Vung Tau, First Sergeant Peck had made arrangements for the soldiers from our company to house with a civilian military contractor who lived in a French style villa in town. The structure was quite large and had rooms for up to 10 people to sleep. There was no air conditioning, but the villa had 12 foot ceilings and louvered shutters all around the outside of the building so you could

U. S. Military R&R Center and beach at Vung Tau
(Rooms were in short supply and most soldiers stayed at homes or hotels in the area)

Looking towards the northeast up the beach at Vung Tau

The beach at the port area around the point from the main beach at Vung Tau
(Note all the ships in the background waiting to go up the Saigon River to unload their cargo)

Helicopter view coming into Vung Tau with the Saigon River below us

A bird's eye view of the Vietnamese coastline

adjust the ventilation to avail yourself of the local breezes. When we first arrived at the villa we were assigned our sleeping areas, and then we were off to explore the town and check on the local bars and clubs. Later that evening after we had gotten back to the villa, a mama-san brought her girls over so we could select our companions for the night. I ended up with this extremely attractive, petite girl named Lan who spoke English, and was in her late teens. She was very athletic, and I remember being enthralled by the gymnastic moves that she could make with her body. Apparently Lan was a frequent visitor to the villa because the contractor told me she had really been stunning before she had a baby. I recall getting into a confrontation with him about his attitude; not exactly the best move when you're a house guest. For the rest of my R&R, Lan and I were inseparable, and we spent time exploring the sights, visiting her room, and swimming at the beach. When Lan and I were swimming together, I was having a difficult time seeing the numerous jellyfish that were in the water because I wasn't wearing my glasses. She was hanging on to me and had to keep warning me of any jellyfish that were in our vicinity. The night before I was to return to Cu Chi, she was pressing me to set her up in Cu Chi so I could visit with her there. I mulled over her proposition, but there weren't many occasions to mingle with the local population at Cu Chi, and I wasn't feeling very adventurous about having a woman stashed there. I didn't know if she had genuine feelings for me, simply wanted out of her situation in Vung Tau, or was a spy for the Viet Cong. In Vietnam you just never really knew what motives were in the hearts of the locals you came into contact with.

Although the Army provided us with all the items necessary for existence, there was still that touch of home that we all missed. My dad was into his second marriage with his new British wife, Pauline, and they had just moved from England to Wellesley, Massachusetts. Pauline was approximately 10 years older than me, and I didn't really know what to think about the marriage, but when it came to goodie packages from home, Pauline was the queen. Most soldiers received small goodie boxes, but Pauline's were huge in comparison. Her package was crammed with candy, home made baked items like cookies and Scottish scones, and numerous other scarce items that I had requested in my last letter home. Pauline was very inventive at finding new items as well, and one of the things we all enjoyed most was this Salada lemonade mix that was packaged in foil pouches with real sugar in the mix. All we had to do was add water and voila, instant lemonade. When Pauline's package came to our hooch, it was always a major event for all of us as we opened the box and investigated the contents.

725th Maintenance Battalion Soldier of the Month Certificate

MY TOUR COMES TO AN END

In October, I was nominated as "Soldier of the Month" for the entire 725th Maintenance Battalion (approximately 800 soldiers). I got dressed in my best uniform and then traveled to the battalion headquarters where I was to be questioned concerning military protocol and my job functions. A short wait later I was called before the examining board that consisted of the battalion's commander, Lt. Colonel Proudfoot, and other officers from the battalion. I marched into the office, stood at attention, and saluted. After the officers returned my salute, I was instructed to stand at rest and the questioning began. Normally situations like this made me nervous, but by the time of this nomination I had a devil-may-care attitude when it came to the Army. I was loose as a goose and even when I made a mistake, I laughed and corrected myself. When the officers laughed back I started feeling pretty good about this. After the questioning finished, I again came to attention and saluted. After the salute was returned, I wheeled and marched out of the room. The end result was that I was selected as the "Soldier of the Month", given a citation that hangs on my wall to this day, and was given my second 2 day R&R to Vung Tau. On this trip I even received a paid reservation at the R&R Center, and I was soon off for another 2 day tour of Vung Tau's bars and looking for trouble. My first time in Vung Tau I had been with fellow soldiers I knew from Company C, but this time I was on my own and it wasn't as much fun without my buddies to get in trouble with. Because I was an individual, other groups in the bars would try to keep me isolated from the bar's activities just like they were protecting their turf. I had visions of meeting with Lan again, and when I arrived I tried to find her, but was never successful in my attempt. Perhaps she had found some other soldier that was willing to put her up in the vicinity of where his duty assignment was.

As Christmas of 1966 approached, all of the advanced party soldiers that had left Hawaii in 1965 were being sent home early for Christmas. This was true for everyone except four of us that didn't have replacements yet. Of course yours truly was one of the four and I wasn't too enamored with the situation. I was down in the dumps and wasn't picking any bones about it. One of my favorite things that I had acquired a taste for while living in England was drinking Scotch neat, so for Christmas Eve I went to the PX and bought myself a bottle of Scotch; it was Johnny Walker Red if I remember correctly. I took the bottle to our shop area where I managed to finish almost half the bottle. What a sorry sight I was. The end result was my getting sick and completely loosing my love of Scotch for the rest of my life. On Christmas Day most of us were off duty. I'm sure I was hung over, but I was convinced by some of my fellow soldiers to go to Bob Hope's show later in the afternoon. When we got to the amphitheater area at Cu chi, there were already thousands of soldiers who had staked out the best seats and we would have needed binoculars in order to see anything. In addition, the TV film crew had constructed all this scaffolding in front of the stage for use in filming the event. I can recall many of us in the back commenting on how the scaffolding was blocking our view. It seemed to us like the show was planned as a TV moment to show the people back home, and not for the

My final armament shop area - CONEX containers for secured items

soldiers at Cu Chi. We all stayed for the show that featured Bob with Joey Heatherton and other celebrities, but seeing any detail or hearing anything was next to impossible. I do however have the privilege of saying that I saw Bob Hope in person, something that none of my fellow advanced party peers that left early can say.

For me and most soldiers, the worst times in Vietnam were the first and last month. All throughout the first month, everything is new and you're learning how to exist under stressful, challenging conditions. After that first month, everything sort of settles in and the daily routine becomes just another day. I actually enjoyed exploring and the many new adventures, challenges, and experiences that were to be had. We were told what to avoid, but many of us just had to learn on our own. Finally you get to the point where you have 1 month left in your 1 year tour of duty. You've survived for 11 months, and now the officers and NCOs in your company are pressuring you to extend your tour. They are offering you promotion in rank, a bonus leave back to the States, whatever it will take to get you to extend your tour. However the big question on everyone's mind is,

The Cu Chi Base Camp at the end of 1966
(A small city made from wood, sandbags, and canvas)

"Am I going to make it this last month?" There's always that story about the soldier that gets killed during his last day in-country. As the end of "my" tour approached, I was more than ready to leave.

I finally received my orders to leave Vietnam on January 3, 1967, and immediately went to my hooch to pack. I was instructed that I was only allowed to take back what would fit in my duffle bag, so any old uniforms or items that wouldn't be needed at my next duty station were either left in the barracks or sold to the troops who were staying. I packed my camera and other fragile items into used ammo cans, and stuffed them into my duffle bag that was completely full with all sorts of things I was taking back with me. I think my duffle bag weighed about 100 pounds and it was quite a handful for me to carry around. Later that evening I left Cu Chi for the last time and was transported to the troop departure area at Tan Son Nhat Airfield in Saigon. The next morning, after spending the night in the barracks at the departure center, I, along with everyone else on my plane, was herded into a large room with our duffle bags. On the wall there was a very long list of contraband that wasn't allowed to be taken back to the States. We were all told that we would have to clear customs in California, and if we were caught with any of these items we would be liable for court marshal and all that entailed. The officer in charge then told us that he and his staff would be leaving the room, and any soldier that had any of this contraband with them should pile it in the middle of the floor. Before leaving the room they also informed us that anything that was left on the floor wouldn't be used for disciplinary proceedings against the soldier that left it. In a short amount of time there was a pile of items that was approximately 20 feet across and 2 feet tall. After everyone had repacked their duffle bags we lined up to board a Braniff DC8 that the military had chartered to take us back to the States. Braniff's planes were painted in solid bright colors like lemon yellow, orange, lime green, and baby blue with the planes tail painted white with large "B I" lettering in the plane's color. I don't recall what color ours was, but it sure was a pretty plane. As we stood in line to get on the plane, we dropped off our duffle bag to be loaded into the planes cargo hold, and then climbed the boarding stairs to an airplane that was packed 6 across and stem to stern with about 180 soldiers.

My Vietnam Ribbons

On January 4, 1967, our plane rolled down the runway and as we lifted off, I was experiencing my last time on Vietnamese soil. After a 1 hour stopover in Tokyo for refueling, we took off for the long trip across the Pacific to Travis Air Force Base in

California close to San Francisco. When we landed at Travis there was a sense of jubilation on the plane … we had all survived our stint in Vietnam and were looking forward to what came next. After deplaning, we were taken to an area where we claimed our duffle bag and then went through customs. At the customs area they first matched us up with the custom's declaration slips we had filled out during our plane trip. We were all expecting that we might have to pay duty on expensive items we had with us and at a minimum were going to have to repack our duffle bags after they had been examined. Most of us were simply matched up with our declaration and waived on through. Just think of all that contraband I could have smuggled in. After picking up my travel voucher for my trip back to my dad's home in Massachusetts, I got on the bus for the 60 mile ride to San Francisco International Airport. I was so glad to be back in the United States and ready for a 45 day leave.

I arrived at my dad's home in Massachusetts, and here I was in the cold of January and nothing planned for activities. That first day back my dad showed me their alarm system panel and told me not to open the door or windows after he set it and went to bed. With the time difference, I was having a hard time getting to sleep, and trying to find something to keep me occupied. About 02:00 I opened the back door to go out on the patio for some crisp winter air, and the large alarm bell that was located up at the peak of the roof under the eaves immediately sounded and woke everyone in our house as well as most of the neighbors. After my dad had reset the alarm, I think the lesson about not opening the door or windows had finally sunk in, and everyone eventually got back to sleep.

My brother Bruce, who had joined the Air Force in September of 1965, was now stationed as a radar repairman at an air base in the MeKong Delta of Vietnam, and my baby sister Pam, who was still going to high school, was more into doing things with her friends than hanging out with her older brother. My dad was working in Boston during the day, I hardly knew my stepbrother Mark, who was 9 at the time, and my stepmother, Pauline, was friendly enough, but she wasn't responsible for entertaining me. This 45 day leave started to feel like it might have not been the best thought out idea on my part. Perhaps I should have saved the vacation time and gotten paid for it when I got discharged, but at this point I didn't think I could just show up early at my new duty station and get back to work. Unfortunately, I then reverted back to my teen age ways of sleeping late, lying around, watching TV, and eating. Oh yes, Pauline was an excellent cook and we did eat well. Eventually February came around and it was time to pack my duffle bag, get into uniform, travel to my new duty station at Fort Hood, Texas, and finish my Army enlistment. When I got back from Vietnam I weighed about 165 pounds, but during my 45 day leave I had ballooned to 180+ pounds and now my uniform DID NOT fit. Pauline did some quick alterations and we managed to get me squeezed into my travel uniform, but I now knew what my first order of business was going to be when I got to Texas.

25th Infantry Division – 2nd Brigade
Company C - 725th Maintenance Battalion - Cu Chi – October 1966

Capt:
CO: James T. Kennedy
Joe A Lewis
Jose R Santiago

1st. Lt:
Francis J Casieri

CWO3:
Roy H. King

WO1:
Moody C Jenkins

E-8:
FS: James A Peck

E-7:
Joseph McCloskey

E-6:
Javier F Espejo
Oscar O Green
Eddie J. Green
James E Hagler
David Haver
Larry E. Henry
Bobby J. Maier
Bobby G Mansfield
Nathaniel McClendon
Charles E Price
Washiro Shigematsu

E-5:
Charles Adkins
Kenneth Alexander
George Bess III
Robert J. Bouchard
James C. Brown
Joseph Burns
James R. Carroll

Henry A. Corning
Ervin A. Crim
Arcade J. Gauthier
Earl A. Jackson, Jr.
Miles H Maltby
Gene W. Miller
Massie R. Odom
Billy J. Patterson
Billy J. Powell
Woodrow W. Priester
Gerhard H. Pulver
Robert E. Taylor
Wells R. Westover
Harvey F. Young Jr.

E-4:
Gayron L. Allen
William L. Allinger
Larry S. Austin
Thomas A. Baird
Douglas T. Barham
Micheal W. Beach
Larry L. Billetter
John M. Briand
Harvey L. Brown
Harry T. Day
Wayne T. Dewberry
Lawrence Dickinson
Joseph R. Dixon
Joseph L. Duskin, Jr.
Guy E. Easton
John R. Ehlors
David W. Ferry
John J Fiumara
Pedro Garcia
James R. Harris
Ronald W. Head
Albord Hunter, Jr.
Gary H. Kato
Willard L. Kenyon
Ronald C. Kirk
Edward A. Kujawa

Danny L. Ludwiski
Thomas H. Magill, Jr.
Bobby M. McCall
Robert L. McCourt
Emmitte McDaniel
John J. McMahon
Roy C. Miller
Earl E. Mirgon
Robert T. Mollenkof
Francisco Ordaz
Terry W. Peer
Wilbert J. Scott
Richard C. Snyder
Stephen D. Tackett
Robert N. Thompson
Warren D. Welch
Frederick Willard

E-3:
Robert S. Anderson
Robert E. Bradford
Ronald D. Carleton
Fred C. Cheffey
Paul Adarno Colon
Donald C. Deskins
Kenneth Florkowski
Willie L. Fountain
Thomas H. Gerali
Robert Gregg
Micheal C. Herrold
Martin McDermott
Benjamin R. Nelson
John B. Taylor, Jr.
Samuel M. Terry

E-2:
Nelson A. Carhart
Kenneth J. Hitz
David A. Janda
Robert D. Robertson
James W. Sparks

(Information derived from 25th Division 25th Anniversary Yearbook 1941-66)

COMPANY C
725TH MAINTENANCE BATTALION
APO San Francisco 96225

AVTIMNT-C   31 December 1966

SUBJECT: Letter of Appreciation

TO: Specialist Fourth Class (E4) Warren D Welch RA 13845007
    Company C, 725th Maintenance Battalion
    APO 96225

1. It gives me great pleasure to award you this Letter of Appreciation for your outstanding performance of duty as the Senior Artillery Repairman for the past twenty-three months.

2. Your demonstrated performance of duty has been in the highest traditions of your technical specialty. You have been highly instrumental in keeping the artillery, Small Arms and Fire control equipment of the 2nd Brigade operable. Many of these repairs were only possible because of your ingenuity in fabricating items which were non-available and through application of field fix procedures which you initiated. Your efforts are significant contributions to the thousands of men who depend on the armament which you maintain for both their successful operations and survival. Your great desire to provide the best support possible to the forward combat units have brought you in direct contact with the enemy on several occasions.

3. It has been a pleasure to have been associated with you in this work. I am confident that the attributes displayed by you will stand you in good stead in whatever endeavor the future holds for you. I wish you the best of success in the future and extend to you my sincere thanks and appreciation for a task magnificently accomplished.

4. A copy of this letter will be made a permanent part of your 201 file.

THADDEUS E. PINKNEY
CWO (W4)   USA
Armament Repair Technician

Company C Letter of Appreciation

FUN AT FORT HOOD

I flew to Dallas and then took a Trans Texas (Tree Top) prop airplane to Temple, Texas, before taking a bus to Killeen and Fort Hood. When I arrived, I reported for duty at Headquarters & Company A, 124th Maintenance Battalion, 2nd Armored Division and got settled into my new home in the barracks. In Vietnam, a soldier of SP4 rank was towards the bottom of the pecking order and subject to KP and all sorts of menial tasks in addition to your normal day to day duties. At Fort Hood, after one sergeant E-5, I was the ranking person in a barracks full of privates just waiting to be assigned to a permanent duty station which was probably going to be Vietnam. I was assigned a private room at the end of the hall that was next to the bathroom. I wouldn't be participating in KP or latrine duty here; I was going to like this. To make matters even better, I got a raise in monthly pay to $205 at the end of February because I went over 2 years of service. I hadn't gotten my promotion to SP5, but Vietnam was behind me and under the rules of the time, I couldn't be forced to return to Vietnam with my non-critical MOS. I would not see Vietnam again unless I volunteered to return or reenlisted.

With a couple of exceptions, I was really going to like being at Fort Hood. We stood formation at 06:00 and worked until 16:00 with trips to the mess hall at breakfast and lunch breaking up the day. Most days we were left to our own devices after 16:00 and all weekend long. Fort Hood was a large base and had pretty much everything when it came to entertainment for the troops that didn't have a lot of money to spend. There was a bowling alley, the enlisted men's club that only served 3.2 beer so 18 to 20 year olds could drink, a movie theater, and many other facilities. The place I really enjoyed was the roller skating rink, because I could go have a lot of fun as well as get some exercise in an attempt to lose some of the weight I'd gained during my ill planned leave. The roller skating rink was also frequented by many of the NCO's and officers' dependents that were going to high school in Killeen. Many of the younger girls were a temptation to some of the soldiers, but I was never that tempted or foolish. I also experienced my first tassel twirling stripper at the enlisted men's club one evening. You can imagine all the noise with hundreds of soldier's cat calling as she performed her act. Now there's some entertainment that you wouldn't be seeing in today's Army. Off base there were the private clubs at Harker Heights where membership cost $1. In Texas back in the 60s there was no liquor by the drink in restaurants or clubs. To get an alcoholic drink you had to belong to a private club or go to a BYOB (Bring Your Own Bottle) bar where they served beer and wine, and charged you for the glasses and ice for your own bottle. Killeen was a dry city and you had to go outside the city limits to buy any kind of alcohol. Of course the officer's and NCO clubs on Fort Hood had no such restrictions.

When I first got to Fort Hood my top priority was to figure out how to harness this weight thing. A new found buddy and I first went to the gym that was on base and tried lifting weights, but this soon got boring and I didn't feel like it was getting the job done. The roller skating was helping, but I needed more, so when spring and warm weather came along, I started running with some fellow soldiers every afternoon when I got off

In front of my barracks at Ft. Hood in 1967

work at 16:00. We started off at 2 miles, but eventually worked up to 5 miles, and I got to the point where I really enjoyed the runner's high. Between my normal Army duties and the running, I was eventually able to get my weight down to 175 pounds, but nowhere close to what was needed to fit into those suits I'd purchased in Hong Kong.

Because I was assigned to an armored division, most of the artillery, like towed 105s and self-propelled 175s from Vietnam, wasn't available at Fort Hood. There were however lots of M-60-A1 tanks to work on that I never had any training on. Tanks weren't a big item in Vietnam because of conditions there, so most of the tanks at Fort Hood had no troops assigned to them, and they sat empty in long rows in the motor pools of their assigned units. Now some of them were being utilized, but most of them were just sitting there waiting for an appropriate war. At my assigned work area there was a lieutenant in charge, a couple of sergeants, me as an E-4, and about 30 privates. In normal daily operations I didn't have to get my hands on things because I was tasked with watching the privates to make sure they were performing their jobs properly. After having been a man of action and working on my own in Vietnam, this was starting to get pretty boring. When they offered me the chance to be on the battalion's honor guard, I jumped at the chance. Instead of following a bunch of 18 year old privates around, I got to dress up and participate in some pageantry by practicing marching drills most mornings. I was willing to try anything to get this last year of my Army career to hurry along.

Fort Hood is one of the largest military installations in the world, and has miles of space to conduct training in. Occasionally, we would participate in field exercises so we could practice our maintenance skills and sleep under the stars in our shelter halves. I've been there and done that, but it was a change from the normal routines. Again I was called on

124th Maintenance Batallion honor guard at Ft. Hood, Texas in 1967
(I'm 2nd from the right - we spent a lot of time practicing to get ready for parades and events)

to drive a truck, but this time I got to tow a 2 wheel trailer behind it as well. The trailer was a challenge to back up with at first, but I soon got fairly proficient with it. On one operation we were going down some very steep hills on a dirt trail somewhere in the boonies. I put my truck in first gear, low range, and still had to use my brakes to keep from running into the truck that was in front of me in the convoy. When the exercise was over and we arrived back at our motor pool area, all the trucks were very muddy so the first order of business was to get the trucks washed. I got the trailer disconnected and then headed over to the wash rack. The first time I pressed the brake pedal, it went all the way to the floor and I had to use my emergency brake to get stopped. It appears that during the field exercise, the flexible brake line leading to the right front wheel had snagged on something and been damaged. The defect had finally failed and dumped all the brake fluid on the ground. Army vehicles of the time did not have a dual chamber brake master cylinder (separate front and rear brake fluid reservoirs), so loss of your brake fluid meant you had no brakes at all. In fact, it wasn't until 1968 when the government mandated that civilian automobiles had to have a dual chamber brake master. Who knows how long it took the military to get their trucks retrofitted? We were all speculating as to what could have happened if this had occurred while we were going down that steep hill during the exercise. With the extra weight of my trailer, the emergency brake might have not been enough to get the truck stopped. It sure is funny how things work out in your favor sometimes.

Clothes display in barracks
Always ready for inspection

One of the things I liked least at Fort Hood was standing formation in front of the barracks at 06:00 when it was 32 degrees with a light drizzle falling. Texas was the coldest climate that I was stationed at, and the winter weather was miserable at times. I made a mental note to myself that I would never live in Texas. Never say never because I've now been living in Texas since 1973, or over half my life. The other thing I didn't like was being assigned to the Fort Hood Base Emergency Reactionary Force for a period of time. This was a pain in the butt because you always had to have your gear at the ready, and they would sometimes wake you up at 03:00 to have you run around acting like someone had just attacked the base. Of course we had no ammunition, so a real attack would have posed a problem.

Some of my fellow soldiers had cars while they lived in the barracks; in fact there were parking lots for your personal car just in front of the barracks. I had a license and was approved to drive Army vehicles, but my personal driver's license was the one I'd gotten in England and it had expired while I was in Vietnam. I talked one of my friends into taking me to the Texas Department of Public Safety's office close by the base so I could take my written test to get my Texas driver's license. Now I had initially received my driver's license when I was 15 in Maine, so how difficult could this be? I sat down, took the test without ever having cracked the manual on Texas Driving Laws, and failed miserably. It seemed like half the test was about DUI laws in Texas, and what did this have to do with my driving? My friend who had taken me to get the license was ribbing me badly about having failed the test. Fortunately there was no waiting period before you were allowed to retake the test, so I took the manual back to the barracks, and after a few hours of studying, I went back and passed the test. Now I was legal to drive in Texas.

After a few months at Fort Hood I began to realize that I had some disposable income, so I decided it was time to get myself a car. Most of the soldiers at the base were driving or looking for muscle cars like Mustangs, Cameros, or Chevelle SS-396s. I on the

My first new car - a 1967 Opel Kadet
(I'm on the right)(My car payments were $65 a month for 3 years)

other hand had been brought up driving small cars with a manual transmission like a Volkswagen Karman Ghia, Ford Anglia, or Austin Mini. I went to the Buick dealer in Killeen looking for a used car that would fit my budget, but when I got there I discovered they were also dealers for Opels, small GM cars that were made in Germany. On the lot they had a brand new bright yellow Opel Kadet that had just been in a hail storm and sustained superficial damage. It was the end of the model year for Opel, and because of the hail damage, I got the car for $1,800 and financed it with GMAC for $65 per month. My soldier based, high risk insurance with Dairyland Mutual cost about $20 a month additional, but with gas at 25 cents per gallon, I was paying for my independence. This was my first new car, and I loved it. The yellow Kadet was eye catching, especially after I added a black racing stripe. It was fun to drive; was reliable transportation; and got over 30 miles per gallon. Having a car also made you popular in the barracks because most of the privates didn't have their own car.

When you lived on base, the area where you slept was always subject to being inspected. This meant folding and rolling all your clothing to military specs and displaying your items in a prescribed manner. There were many items that you constantly had to be redoing because as you washed your clothes you had to get them ready for inspection when they came back from the laundry. If you had a car however, you could purchase extra items and store them in your car's trunk for your day to day use. The items in your bunk area were always ready for inspection and never had to be redone.

Cars from the time before computers were very mechanical and infinitely less electronic than the cars of today. Most boys of the time learned how to work on cars in their

Drag racing in my Opel at Temple, Texas in 1967

Drag Racing Trophies

teenage years, and like many people I did most of my own maintenance like changing the oil and tuning my car. In addition, the Army maintained a fully equipped shop area complete with an instructor for the soldiers' use in maintaining or overhauling their private cars during their off duty hours. I went to Gibson's Discount Center in Killeen and purchased a mechanics manual, timing light, points file, and many other tools and items to keep my car tuned to perfection. I was bound and determined to make a hot rod out of my car even if it only had a 1200cc engine under the hood. On Sundays many of the Fort Hood soldiers, especially the ones with fast cars, would head to Temple-Academy Dragway in Temple, Texas to compete in drag racing and see how their car would perform. After one visit to check things out, I got the bug and decided to join them in a quest to get as much speed out of my little car as possible. I bought racing spark plugs, a high performance coil, and learned how to modify the distributor in order to maximize the horse power of my car's engine. I also went to a muffler shop in Killeen and put a cut-out on the exhaust pipe so I could bypass the muffler when I was racing. My Opel Kadet raced in N stock class (the slowest class) and I competed against cars like Volkswagen Beatles, VW 1500 Fastbacks, Corvair sedans, and early 50's era Ford sedans with a flathead V8. The cars that gave me the most problem were the VW Fastback and one particular Corvair, but by the time they closed the track for the winter of 1967, I had won 17 trophies. I got to thinking that my car was really fast for N-Stock, so one weekend I decided to go to Austin and race at the NHRA sanctioned track. This was where the big boys raced at, and my Opel was soon sent packing. I couldn't afford to take the car that I depended on for transportation and do what it would take to convert it into a car that might have been competitive on the big stage.

My brother, Norman Bruce Welch, at the spring in Del Rio, Texas in 1967

Having my Opel also allowed me to explore many areas of Texas that were close to Fort Hood like Austin, Dallas, San Antonio, and Waco. It allowed me to see the Alamo, the Texas Ranger Hall of Fame and Museum, Dealey Plaza, and many other sights that Texas has to offer. On weekends during the summer we would often go swimming at Lake Belton, but you had to be careful not to drink alcoholic beverages at the county park before noon on Sunday because the sheriff's deputies would throw you in jail. Twice I drove to Del Rio for the weekend to see my brother Bruce who was then stationed at Laughlin Air Force Base. I would bring a couple of friends from Fort Hood and we would all head across the Mexican border to "Boys Town" to see what trouble we could find. On a 2 day weekend we were not supposed to travel more than 200 miles, but one of my college friends had set me up with a friend of his who lived in Shreveport, Louisiana.

Judy had taken a job there after graduating from Denver University. I was all up for some female companionship, but the trip involved traveling almost 300 miles. After weighing the risks, I started making a weekly jaunt to visit with Judy in Shreveport. This worked for a while, but soon got old because I couldn't see the relationship going anywhere. I don't think I even called her to let her know I wasn't coming back anymore; maybe I wrote her? After all, long distance calls were expensive at the time.

In November they had me take proficiency tests to see how well I had learned my duties in my 45C20 MOS. When I was taking the test many of the questions were about weapons that I hadn't seen or even thought about since I graduated from AIT over two years earlier. Fortunately I've been blessed with a good memory, and I recalled enough information concerning these artillery pieces to max out every section of the test. Passing this test meant another $40 a month, and additionally I was now put up for promotion to SP5 E-5. After going before the review board on November 21st, I finally got the promotion I could have gotten a year earlier if I'd just extended my tour in Vietnam. But here I was, living in the barracks within the borders of the United States with all my room and board taken care of, and in addition I was now getting paid over $300 a month. Army life was starting to look pretty good, and I had a lot to think about. With the end of my enlistment now pending in February of 1968, the officers and sergeants of Company A started hitting me hard about reenlisting. I planned on going back to college when finished with the Army, and a reenlistment bonus would have helped with that goal. They also offered to make me a warrant officer, which would have been a promotion and given me recognition as a technical expert and specialist. This was all enticing, but I knew that reenlisting probably meant a return to duty in Vietnam and I'd had all I wanted of that situation. I just kept biding my time and finally received my orders to be mustered out of active duty. After taking a physical exam, verifying to the Army that I was in good shape, and signing my discharge papers, I was given my freedom on February 23, 1968, and I drove my Opel Kadet off into the sunset. I had already been accepted back at the University of Denver and was anxious to get back to school after a brief trip to see my mom in Pennsylvania and my dad in Massachusetts.

MOS EVALUATION DATA REPORT (AR 600-200-AR 135-205)	5 JAN 68	USAEEC EVALUATION PERIOD NOV 67	TCO SYMBOL 228	REFERENCE ROSTER NUMBER P 5059

SECTION 1. INDIVIDUAL EVALUATED.

THRU: COMMANDING OFFICER
0124 MAINT BN
HOOD FT   TX

WELCH WARREN D

MOS IN WHICH EVALUATED	MOS EVALUATION SCORE
45C20	144

GRADE - PAY GRADE - PPD	SERVICE NUMBER
SP4 E-4	RA 13 845 007

SECTION 2. INDIVIDUAL'S MOS EVALUATION TEST PROFILE.

SUBJECT MATTER AREA (DA PAM 12-45C. DATED JUN 67)	VERY LOW	LOW	TYPICAL	HIGH	VERY HIGH
105-MM HOWITZERS					X
155-MM HOWITZERS					X
8-INCH HOWITZERS					X
318-MM RL & 762-MM TRUCK-MOUNTED RL					X
BORE EVALUATION, GAS PRESSURE TEST & ARTY AMMO					X
USE TOOLS GAGES EQUIP PUB & REC SYS					X

EPEECO FORM 10   1 AUG 67   EDITION OF 1 AUG 65 MAY BE USED   DISTRIBUTION: ORIGINAL - INDIVIDUAL'S 201 FILE / FIRST COPY - INDIVIDUAL EVALUATED / SECOND COPY - SPECIAL

FIRST COPY

45C20 MOS Evaluation Test Scores

WELCH, WARREN D RA13845007 (   ) SP5 E5 P45C20 HQ & Co A 124th Maint
Bn 2d Armd Div Ft Hood TX 76546 Fourth US Army
   Res asg: USAR Con Gp (Reinf W-81U) USAAC St Louis MO 63132
   Res-SN, gr, basic br, comp: ER13845007 SP5 E5 Ord C USAR
   HOR: 318 West Johnson St, Philadelphia, PA
   Perm adrs: 78 Ivy Rd, Wellesley, MA 02181
   P1 EAD: Same as HOR (P1 Enl)
   Last perm dy sta: Ft Hood Texas, Fourth US Army   C-1-23
   VRB dsg: NA
   ACLV: 8 days
   No yrs svc pay gr E4: NA
   UMTS Act oblg: 6 yrs
   SPN: 201
   BASD: 26 Feb 65
   EDCSA (REFRAD): 2400 hrs, 23 Feb 68

Final Army Separation Orders

Looking down the barrel of an M-107 175mm self-propelled artillery gun. This gun had a 33 kilometer range with high explosive rounds. The photo was taken in 1966 at the Cu Chi basecamp of the 25th Infantry Division by Warren D. Welch, Company C, 725th Maintenance Battalion. It was SP4 Welch's duty to periodically inspect the barrel with a bore sight to insure the safety of this powerful weapon.

Archive Photo courtesy of Warren D. Welch

25th Infantry Division Association Calendar Pictures

25th Division Artillery supports infantry operations near the Ho Bo Woods northwest of Cu Chi in 1966.   *Archive Photo by Warren D. Welch*

IN CONCLUSION

In the Army some of the phrases we used regarding various situations were "F**k the Army" (FTA for the short form), "Close enough for government work," "Hurry up and wait," and "If it doesn't fit, get a bigger hammer." We called the Viet Cong, "Charlie" or "VC," a medical helicopter evacuation, "dustoff," an infantryman, "grunt," and living quarters, "hooch." You were "gung ho" if you were enthusiastic, used "rock n roll" to mean firing your weapon in full automatic mode, and "lock and load" meant to lock the magazine into place and load a round into the chamber. The Vietnamese used expressions that we adopted like "bookoo" for many, "boom boom" for sex with a soldier, "dinky dau" for crazy, and "di di mau" for move quickly. This was a whole new way of expressing yourself and communicating with everyone around you.

Many soldiers in Vietnam didn't have much respect or use for the Vietnamese people and their culture that we were there fighting for. They were disrespectful at times and used derogatory names like "Gooks" or "Slopes" when they referred to the Vietnamese people. Now this always made me uncomfortable when I was around soldiers talking like this, but I never said anything because I wasn't looking for confrontation. A lot of this was from soldiers who felt forced into the Vietnam situation, but also came from older soldiers who had experienced the military culture from the Korean War. Many of us seemed to forget that this was their country, and we were just visitors along for the ride. Ultimately we were leaving and they were going to have to figure things out for themselves.

One thing that aggravates me, even today, is when someone tells me that they wish they'd gone to Vietnam, and I know damn well that, at the time, they chose to do everything in their power to avoid going. I have more respect for my cousin that declared as a conscientious objector and worked in a VA hospital than I do for them. Without being rude, I just don't know how to answer them. If they didn't feel a sense of duty to their country back then, then why are they now telling me that they wish they had gone? For the most part we were just a bunch of young guys running around in a foreign country doing what our country was asking us to do. Those who chose to avoid putting all at risk will never really understand what being in Vietnam was like.

I've had people tell me I was lucky to survive going to Vietnam, but the reality is that there were millions of us that went, and most of us returned. I don't know the actual statistics, but I was told that the 725th Maintenance Battalion experienced only 1 casualty out of its 800 or so men for all of 1966. Personally I would attribute this to the fact that we were a support battalion, 1966 was early in the war, Cu Chi base camp suffered no major attacks from the Viet Cong or North Vietnamese Army in 1966, and the enemy wasn't using 107mm and 122mm Chinese made rockets yet. While I was at Fort Hood I heard that Cu Chi experienced attacks from the Viet Cong and NVA in 1967 after I left, and they also started experiencing rocket attacks which would have been a game changer as far as I'm concerned.

In Vietnam, my best friend was Guy Easton, the small arms repairman. He had been drafted, was very vocal about his dislike of military life, and talked about his dreams of becoming a gunsmith in civilian life when he got out. When he left in December of 1966 his 2 year active duty commitment to the Army was finished, and he was assigned to the Army Reserve when he got back to California. We lost track of each other after Vietnam, and when I was able to track him down some 30 years later, I was surprised when he told me he had reenlisted around 1969 and gone back to Vietnam. In my wildest dreams, Guy would have been the last person I would pick to volunteer to go back into the Army. As I have lived my life after leaving the Army I look back on my military experience with a sense of accomplishment and a gratitude for giving me a mind set where I could tackle any obstacle or problem and conquer it. As I returned to college, I did get treated badly on a few occasions, and some younger people didn't trust me because I had been to Vietnam, but by ignoring their short sighted attitudes and taking the high road, I proved that I would win in the lottery of life. I am proud that I went to Vietnam and served my country.

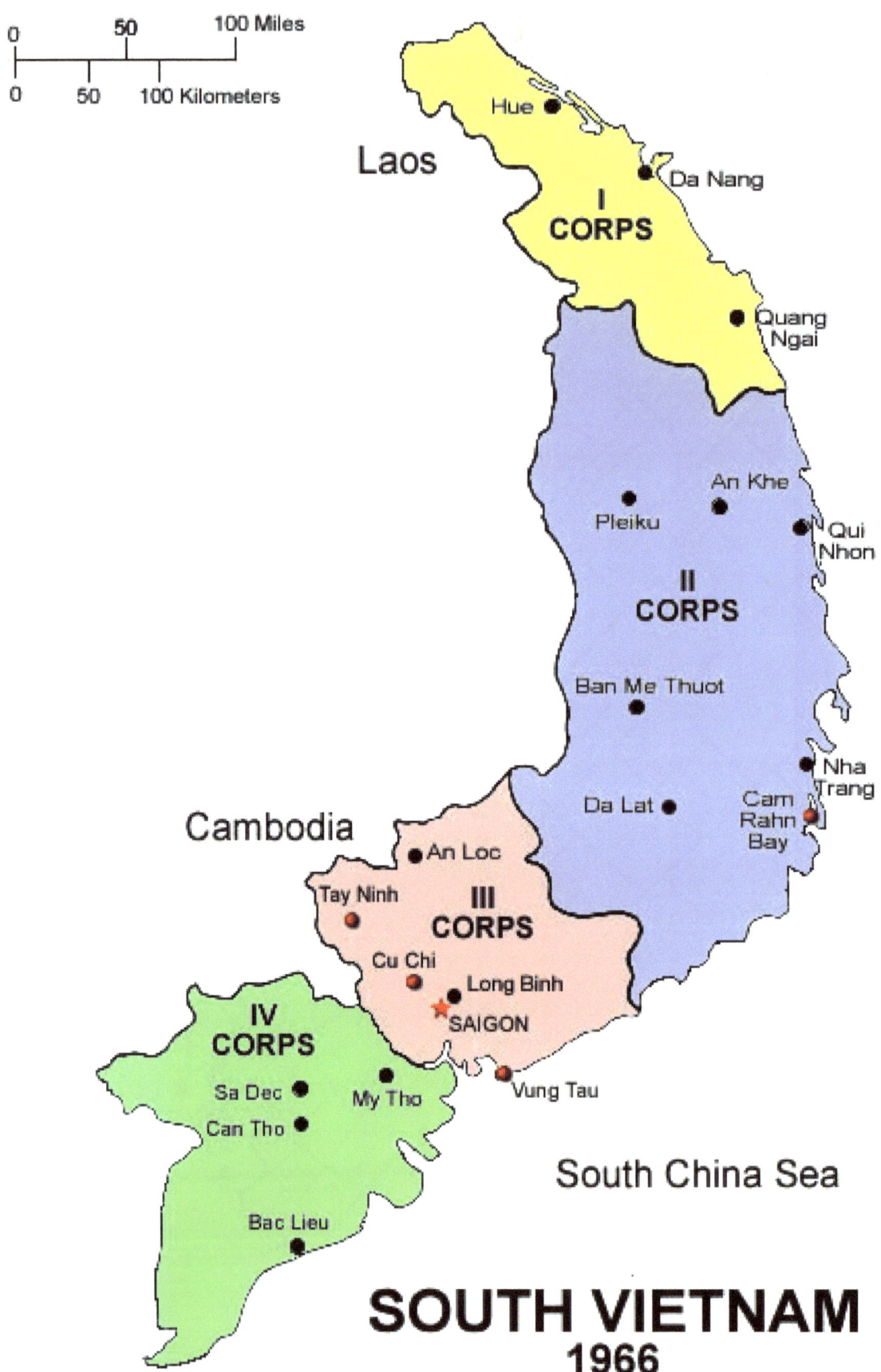

JOHN "MAC" MCMAHON – A COOK'S PERSPECTIVE

I was born in Hoosick Falls, N.Y., and graduated from high school at the age of 16. I tried to join the Navy but was turned down because at the age of 9 I broke my arm and

John McMahon in front of his hooch at Cu Chi   John with some of the locals at Cu Chi
Photos compliments of John McMahon

it wasn't set correctly. At the age of 22 I was drafted and took Basic Training at Fort Dix in New Jersey. Three weeks into Basic I got double pneumonia and my weight dropped to 127 pounds. I then had the misfortune of having to start Basic over, and had my MOS changed from clerk typist to cook. I took my cook AIT at Fort Dix as well.

I got stationed at Schofield Barracks, Hawaii, and loved being there even if it was only for two months. The cooks had separate quarters on Lanai because of the early hours they worked to get the food ready. I got to travel to Waikiki on a few afternoons after the noon meal was finished. On January 4, 1966, we left for Vietnam on the USNS Gen. Nelson M. Walker. I was terribly seasick the first two days of my voyage so they had me making coffee. One of the soldiers on board was accidentally shot with a personal weapon and we had to make an emergency stopover in Guam to drop him off at the U.S. Naval Hospital. All the troops on board loved watching reruns of old "Combat" TV shows on deck at night. I use ice in all my drinks now because there wasn't a cold drink to be had on that ship.

On January 18th we anchored three miles off the Vietnamese coast at Vung Tau. After being ferried ashore, I was flown to Bien Hoa in an Air Force C-130, and then shuttled to a staging area at Long Binh. After a couple days I was transported to Cu Chi where we had to cook barbeque style for a couple weeks because the mess equipment hadn't arrived yet. I was lucky because I only had to pull guard duty one time during my tour. I got used to mortar attacks and one time I slept right through the attack. I had to pick shrapnel out of tomato and peanut butter cans after an early morning mortar attack, so I sent a piece home in a letter, but it must have gotten lost in the mail because my Mom never got it. The closest I got to getting shot was when we took friendly fire near the mess tent one day. We were told that some VC had gotten between our soldiers out on a recon mission and Cu Chi's perimeter. I helped cook the Thanksgiving meal of 23 turkeys at Tay Ninh, and then flew by Huey back to Cu Chi to set up the mess hall ahead of the returning company. That flight was the only time I got scared in Vietnam.

I got to visit Saigon twice. The first time was with Sergeant Shigematsu, and he set up my first encounter with a young girl named Mai. The next time I went alone, and checked into a hotel, went sightseeing, and forgot the name of the hotel. After racking my brain I finally remembered that it was the Sonata. For my out-of-country R&R, I went to Kuala Lumpur, Malaysia, with Roy Miller. I got drunk for the first time ever and left Roy with Peggy Woo and Penny Sai. I got in a car with a Malaysian girl and ended up at a home in God knows where. The next day I met up with a Staff Sergeant and an airman at breakfast somewhere and then took a cab back to the hotel. When I got back to the hotel, I checked my wallet and noticed it was a little bit short. Oh well! Roy had visions of my demise and he notified the authorities that I was missing. They didn't seem too concerned and told him to let them know if I didn't show up. After arriving in Saigon, I traveled back to Cu Chi in an APC with the driver hell bent on scaring all the locals on the way.

Sergeant Shigematsu kept a bazooka on our mess hall for decoration, but I never saw any ammo for it. We also fermented fruit juice for moonshine. I got to meet Mel Allen the Yankee announcer, and he signed a company glove for me. At the end of my tour I made it to mid-night mass on Christmas Eve, and the Bob Hope show. What I remember most is the guys I lived and worked with, and the kids of Cu Chi. Marty McDermott and I went to Cu Chi a few times and made friends with some of the kids. The kids were great and very polite, and they invited us into their homes to meet Mama San. To this day I worry about what happened to them. I don't think we lost the war, but it was the attitudes at home that cost us the victory. I will never forget my year in Vietnam. I was only a cook, but a damned proud one.

Mac's Selfie taken at the Sonata Hotel, Saigon

Preparing Thanksgiving Dinner at Tay Ninh, Vietnam

James Brown

John McMahon

John "Mac" McMahon's Candid Photos from Cu Chi

725th Maintenance Batallion, Company C
(Picture taken from the mess hall)

MAIL CALL